BERLITZ®

ALGARVE

1987/1988 Edition

By the staff of Berlitz Guides
A Macmillan Company

 Library of Congress Catalog Card No. 79-92933.

Printed in Switzerland by Weber S.A., Bienne.

15th Printing
1987/1988 Edition

How to use our guide

- All the practical information, hints and tips that you will need before and during the trip start on page 101, with a complete rundown of contents on page 104.
- For general background, see the sections The Province and the People, p. 6, and A Brief History, p. 14.
- All the sights to see are listed between pages 24 and 70, with a special section on Lisbon on pages 71 to 79. Our own choice of sights most highly recommended is pinpointed by the Berlitz traveller symbol.
- Entertainment, nightlife and all other leisure activities are described between pages 80 and 91, while information on restaurants and cuisine is to be found on pages 92 to 100.
- Finally, there is an index at the back of the book, pp. 126–128.

Although we make every effort to ensure the accuracy of all the information in this book, changes occur incessantly. We cannot therefore take responsibility for facts, prices, addresses and circumstances in general that are constantly subject to alteration. Our guides are updated on a regular basis as we reprint, and we are always grateful to readers who let us know of any errors, changes or serious omissions they come across.

Text: Ken Bernstein
Photography: Jürg Donatsch
Layout: Doris Haldemann
We are particularly grateful to Luis Rocha and the Portuguese National Tourist Office for their help in the preparation of this book. We would also like to thank the Comissão de Turismo do Algarve, Faro, and Air Portugal for their valuable assistance.

Cartography: Falk-Verlag, Hamburg.

Contents

Maps

The Province and the People

Portugal's southernmost province has enough sandy beaches to toast every sunbather in Europe: delectable secluded coves and great golden strands stretch to infinity. The ocean is the Atlantic but the Algarve feels Mediterranean.

In villages of squat white houses, gnarled old women wearing felt hats hide from the sun under black umbrellas. When the itinerant milkman honks his horn, customers bring their jars to be filled from his churns. Fishermen repaint their boats in colours nearly as bright as the flowers on cliffs above the beach. A knife sharpener, advertising his business on a flute, walks his bicycle through narrow cobbled streets. Two donkey-carts make a traffic jam. At this pace even the most frazzled businessman soon unwinds.

The south coast—about 100 miles of beaches for all tastes—is neatly divided. The western half, its beaches framed by cliffs and surrealistic rock formations, looks like a struggle between Portugal and the Atlantic. But the eastern half is a harmonious marriage of coast and ocean; an intimate coexistence of gentle sands and shoreline sloping up through pines, mimosa, eucalyptus and heather to an altitude of nearly 3,000 feet. These highlands on the southern exposure are the great "plus" for holidaymakers and farmers alike.

The climate is the best in Portugal and, some locals insist, one of the kindest in the world. The Algarve basks in over 3,000 hours of sunshine a year, more than almost any other international resort area.

In summer this may inspire frequent dips in the Atlantic or the hotel pool. But in winter the sun, and the moderating effect of the Gulf Stream, maintain conditions that would qualify as springtime anywhere else.

Normally but a distant dream, snow has a place in the Algarve's most charming legend. During the long Moorish occupation of the country, it is said the ruler fell in love with a beautiful slave (or princess, in another version) who arrived from a far-off northern land. They were married and she tried to adjust to her new life, but nostalgia for the snows of home led her to fall into a slow decline. When the wise king learned the cause of her sadness, he ordered a forest of almond trees to be planted everywhere in sight

Shore chores occupy fishermen at elegant resort town of Albufeira.

of his Algarve castle. The next February, he awakened his beautiful bride from her melancholy sleep and carried her to the window. The fields were white. The sea of almond blossoms, the gift of her loving king, cured her malaise in one brilliant flash.

And if you come to the Algarve in late January or February you can share the wonder and joy. The local poet, Candido Guerreiro (1871–1954), summed up the annual miracle thus:

Em fevereiro, quando lá de cima
Deus, com tinta de luar, escreve
Seus lindos versos algarvios, rima
A flor das amendoeiras com a
neve...

(When in February from heaven/God writes his Algarve poetry in moonlight/His beautiful verses rhyme/The blossoms of the almond trees with snow.)

The romantic husband in the legend was one of many Moorish kings who ruled the Algarve for five centuries. The Moslems, who conquered Iberia in A.D. 711, were finally expelled from the Algarve in the 12th and 13th centuries by Portuguese armies and allied Crusaders. But the Moorish legacy lingers on in many corners of local life. Even the names are Arabic—Algarve, Albufeira, Aljezur, Bensafrim, Quelfes...

After the reconquest and armed with the latest technology, Portugal's 15th-century explorers laid the foundations for the future empire. They were mobilized by Prince Henry the Navigator, whose centre of operations was the Algarve. In fact, the first bold ventures into uncharted seas—opening the golden age in which the Portuguese flag would be first to circle the world—were largely financed by Henry's royalties from the Algarve fishing industry.

The Algarve's destiny as a tourist destination was not thought about until very modern times. Illustrious visitors of the Middle Ages took the waters at the Monchique spa, as the Romans before them, but no one imagined that the Algarve's beaches and sunshine would lure travellers from distant countries and even other continents. By the time the age of mass tourism arrived, well into the second half of the 20th century, most of the mistakes which marred other countries' *costas* had been learned. With a few awkward exceptions, tourist development in the Algarve has been carefully planned, sparing the scenery and the culture.

Bildarchiv Kh. Schuster, Frankfurt

The countryside, with flowering orchards, undulating fields of grain and even lush rice paddies, shows the continuing importance of agriculture to the economy. The beauty of it all is merely a bonus—as is the taste of freshly picked figs, melons, strawberries and grapes.

Graceful blossoms of the almond tree—Algarve's springtime glory.

For centuries fishing has been intimately linked with life on the Algarve. Wherever you go on the coast you'll be alongside fishermen, either the crews of small boats who work just off-shore or the trawlermen who go far out into the ocean in pursuit of the big schools. Salt pans along the eastern Algarve coast have made fish-preserving an easy matter since primitive times. Then, about 100 years ago, the first canneries opened. Millions of the familiar tins of tuna and sardines on supermarket shelves around the globe originate here.

Even if you're not doing any cooking, you'll want to inspect the local fish market wherever you're staying. Just follow your nose to the abundance of fresh, beautiful bream, sole, sardines, and slightly sinister-looking eels and octopi. At any fishing port you can watch them auction the catch. The bargaining is serious—but not to the exclusion of wry interplay between the sellers and buyers.

A Tale of Tile

Everywhere you go in Portugal you'll see *azulejos*, multi-coloured enamelled tile squares which recall the centuries of Moorish occupation. *Azulejos* are classless. They cover the walls of palaces and cottages alike. Of course, the humbler variety are usually industrially produced.

The name itself may derive from the Arabic *az-zulayj* ("little stone"). Another school of thought prefers a simpler root, the Portuguese word *azul* (blue). Early tiles were blue and white.

The Moors who brought the *azulejos* to the Iberian peninsula in the Middle Ages may have borrowed the techniques and geometric designs from the Persians. Portugal's first *azulejos* date from the 16th century. By the 17th blue-and-white had regained favour.

Inside many Portuguese churches large mosaics of tile squares take the place of tapestries. They are decorated with flowery abstractions or form tableaux depicting biblical incidents. The inner walls of palaces and monasteries may be covered with panels composed of landscapes, hunting scenes or fables in cartoon form.

The panels rescued from old mansions or gardens, now considered important antiques, are priced accordingly. But you can buy hand-painted modern versions with traditional or light-hearted designs. A single square—perhaps showing an Algarve chimney, a folklore costume or a Portuguese crowing cock—is as cheap a souvenir as you'll find. Or you can buy a whole ensemble of *azulejos* to enliven your patio or kitchen.

Shopping is part of the fun —for bread and cheese for your picnic, or for souvenirs. You'll be offered the silliest straw hat, or a set of 17th-century blue glazed tiles *(azulejos)* that could cost more than your whole holiday. All the towns have market days at least once a month to which farmers bring their livestock to trade, and artisans and itinerant vendors sell pottery, hand-knitted jerseys and home-made sweets.

With all those beaches, swimming and sailing are the most favoured outdoor activities. But the Algarve also boasts half a dozen golf courses of international calibre and there are facilities for tennis and horseback riding.

The most convenient way of getting around is by car, though the bus system presents

In the 18th-century palace of Estoi near Faro, traditional blue-and-white tiles cover a wall.

a reasonable alternative. It's cheap and usually comfortable. Or you can take the wide-gauge train, with vistas even more unspoiled than the scene from the highways. Sightseeing is a pleasure because of the relatively short distances, uncrowded roads and agreeable distractions: hamlets of blinding white houses with red tile roofs and minaret-shaped chimneys; gardens aflame with bougainvillea and hibiscus; windmills and water-wheels; country women doing the laundry on the riverbank.

The major attractions are towns that recall centuries of adventure, triumph and disaster. Only a handful of monuments still survive from before the year 1755, when almost everything in the Algarve was wiped out by an earthquake. Even so, you'll find vestiges of the Romans, the Moors and the golden age of Portuguese discovery. And even the most unprepossessing village offers

In a shady corner of field near Olhão, countryman and wife share simple pleasure of a picnic lunch.

something to remember—a white church with a classic portal, a market full of excitement, a sleepy plaza shaded by sky-blue jacaranda blossoms.

After a full day's visiting there's more to come. The nightlife starts at outdoor tables where you can have a drink and watch the crowds and the sea. Or you can wander down to the neighbourhood café-cum-billiard-parlour, where the locals don't let foreign influences disturb them—except when a bikini ambles in. Restaurants range from the most elementary sardine-griller (which may turn out to be the highlight of your holiday) to fancy international establishments. You can maintain the momentum at *boîtes* and discos up and down the coast, or sample the floor show and the baccarat, blackjack and roulette at one of the Algarve's cosmopolitan casinos.

The modest, dignified people of the Algarve are notable for their generosity. Strangers may find them laconic but they're always helpful and kind. They're also considerate to animals: house pets and working animals are well looked after, nicely groomed donkeys are decked out in handsomely decorated halters; in Portugal even bullfighters are forbidden to kill the bull.

From Cape St. Vincent to the Spanish border, for swingers or families, the beautiful Algarve and its proud, industrious people are the ingredients for the kind of holiday worth repeating.

A Brief History

Not much is known about the earliest inhabitants of Europe's southwestern extremity. The ancient Greeks called the people the Cynetes or Cunetes. Whoever they were, their habits and beliefs evolved under the pressure of powerful foreign influences. Among invading armies which contributed to the process were Phoenicians, Celts, Iberians, Greeks and Carthaginians.

But the Romans, who arrived in the 3rd century B.C., influenced Portugal more than all their predecessors combined. They built towns, industries, roads and bridges. They imported the Latin language, of which Portuguese is a direct descendant. And in the 3rd century A.D. they introduced Christianity. By the beginning of the 4th century, church records show, the Algarve had a bishop, based in Faro. But Rome was in decay, and soon hordes of northern tribesmen overran the empire. The Algarve fell under the Visigoths in the mid-5th century.

In A.D. 711, powerful armies of North African Moors launched a devastating amphibious attack on the Iberian peninsula. The tide of Islam, which proved irresistible for several centuries, was to leave an indelible influence on the countryside and the population of the Algarve: the agricultural system, the wells and waterwheels, the squat white houses, the complexion—and perhaps some of the complexes—of the people. The Moors also gave the Algarve its name: *Al Gharb* meaning "western land"; from their point of view it was the westernmost country of all.

Under Moslem Rule

The Moors governed Portugal from across the border in Seville. But the Algarve had its own regional capital, the prosperous port city called Chelb. (The name has since been changed to Silves.) Medieval Chelb was bigger than Lisbon and better defended; its fortress was considered invulnerable. Today the town has become a simple provincial outpost with an enviable hillside setting. Its once-proud citadel is now the scene of, among other events, an annual beer festival.

The long struggle to expel the Moors began towards the end of the 8th century, but it

Moorish fortress oversees easy pace of life in once-great Silves.

wasn't until the 12th century that a significant gain was made. The Moslems were routed at the Battle of Ourique in 1139. The commander of the triumphant troops, Count Afonso Henriques, became the first king of Portugal.

The reconquest of Chelb/ Silves, 50 years later, was a

major military operation. Portugal's second king, Sancho I, recruited a mixed bag of Crusaders from northern Europe while they were in transit through Lisbon. The forces sailed to the Algarve to besiege Silves. Conditional offers of surrender were rejected; the Crusaders were out for blood—and booty. When the Moslem fortress capitulated, the devastation on all sides was ghastly, first from the fighting and immediately afterwards from the looting. Whole palaces simply vanished as triumphant soldiers seized the spoils.

Two years later the Moslems geared up for a massive counter-assault and Silves, recaptured, became Chelb again. For another half-century the Portuguese struggled to reconquer all of the Algarve. By then the situation was clouded by a feud between Portugal and Spain, each claiming sovereignty over the region. But the Pope's intervention in 1253, and a token royal marriage, averted war and the "Kingdom of Portugal and the Algarve" became a reality.

The kings of Portugal were to carry the additional responsibility for the Kingdom of the Algarve for hundreds of years, until the monarchy itself was overthrown in 1910. The idea of the Algarve as a separate place made some sense. The region was like an island—cut off on the south and west by the Atlantic, on the east by the Guadiana River frontier, and on the north by mountains.

Lagos port honours Prince Henry, mastermind of great discoveries.

Ceuta and Beyond

In 1415 a Portuguese fleet assembled on the river Tagus in Lisbon for a scrupulously planned operation to beat the Moors on their home ground. Crossing the Strait of Gibraltar, the armada attacked and seized the North African city of Ceuta. An illustrious member of the expedition was a young nobleman, half Portuguese and half English, the son of King João I and his wife Philippa, daughter of the Duke of Lancaster. The king, delighted at the valour of his hitherto bookish son, rushed to the Algarve to welcome him back at Tavira and award him the title of Duke of Viseu. He received other titles—Master of the Order of Christ, even Governor of the Algarve—but most remember him as the man who changed the map of the world: Prince Henry the Navigator.

The expedition to Ceuta was the one and only dangerous journey of Henry's life. At the age of 21 he retired to the Algarve, not for the sun and natural beauty but to be near the "end of the world". He recruited the best astronomers, cartographers, boat designers and seamen and proceeded to roll back the horizon. Algarve shipwrights produced a successor to the lumbering sail-and-oar-powered craft of the day—the caravelle. It was light, fast and manœuverable; any breeze was enough for a captain to steer it where he wanted to go. And with the new navigational skills it was no longer necessary to stay within sight of land. The only limit was man's courage.

Modern writers are tempted to compare the prince's School of Navigation to a space centre of the late 20th century. But the Portuguese explorers could not rely on scientific proof that there really was land over the horizon. There were no computers to help them plot their voyages and once launched, the 15th-century travellers had no communication with their base, no rescue service, not even the comfort of advice. Still, they ventured past Cape St. Vincent into the unknown. During the prince's lifetime Portuguese caravelles sailed beyond the westernmost point of Africa. The Atlantic islands of Madeira and the Azores were colonized, laying the foundations for the future Portuguese empire.

The traditional site of Prince Henry's base is the Sagres peninsula, where certain old ruins look as if they might have served as "Mission Control". But modern historians believe that the real operational centre was in Lagos (25 miles away), which had a port, shipyards and a ready-made home for the prince—the palace of the governor of the Algarve. Hard-headed scholars also play down the concept of a "School of Navigation", which they consider something of an exaggeration or an outright myth. They say it was more like a school of thought than an actual academy. Knowledge was pooled, ventures planned, but classes of sailors never sat through lectures. But school or no school, Sagres or Lagos, everyone acknowledges the achievements of the intrepid Portuguese travellers and the brilliant prince who hired and inspired them.

Prince Henry's crews left "end of world" Algarve for new horizons.

Foreign Intrigues

An unforgettable, untypical Portuguese king was Sebastian (1557–78), who is said to have been deeply moved by the Algarve: the scenery and climate reminded him of North Africa. This helped compound the king's compulsion to conquer Morocco for Christianity. In 1578 he led his army to a confrontation with a much bigger and better Moroccan force in the disastrous battle of Alcácer-Quivir. Along with thousands of his followers, the rash King Sebastian perished. He was 24 years old. For many years afterward, legends and rumours insisted that he had actually survived the battle. Imposters turned up from time to time claiming to be the rightful king; those who were plausible enough to threaten the monarchy were executed.

King Sebastian's sudden end set the stage for a grave national problem. The last surviving son of the great King Manuel, an elderly prince named Henrique, inherited the crown. But he was ill and frail. After less than two years, alternating between throne and sickbed, Henrique died. Celibate to the last, he left no heir. Whereupon the crown was seized by King Philip II of Spain, who invaded Portugal and proclaimed himself the king, Dom Filipe I.

Among the unpleasant aspects of Spanish rule was Portugal's inadvertent involvement in Spain's wars. A British squadron commanded by Francis Drake attacked the Algarve in 1587, when it was considered part of Spain. Lagos resisted but Sagres was sacked. Drake's troops, ignoring the historical importance of Sagres, destroyed almost all the old buildings, thus depriving us of relics of Henry the Navigator. Nine years later another English naval force assaulted Faro, putting the torch to the cathedral and hundreds of other buildings. It was all a far cry from the Treaty of Windsor of 1386 under which Britain and Portugal had pledged eternal and true friendship. Finally, after 60 years of Spanish rule, Portuguese noblemen organized a palace coup in 1640 and independence was restored.

The Great Disaster

Portugal's greatest calamity struck on All Saints' Day, November 1, 1755. With the candlelit churches crowded, the earth shook and rolled. Crumbling ceilings and walls, and fast-spreading fires, killed between 15,000 and 60,000

Kingdom's End

Bloodshed hauntec
few years of the mo
February 1, 1908,
family was riding th
bon's immense rive
za, the Terreiro do
open carriage. An
the crowd murdered
los with a shot in the
other marksman in
spiracy killed the
throne, Prince Lu
His younger broth
Manuel, was hit in
The wounded sur
thus propelled to th
the age of 19. He
been trained for the
failed to distinguis
Amidst republican a
was deposed in 1
uprising by eleme
armed forces. Man
last king of Portugal
for less than three
in exile in 1932 ir
ham, England.

The sudden en
than seven centurie
chy brought a gre
confusion and cri
country. Presidents
ministers, trying to
tion to the unfa
republic, hopped in
of office with disco
quency. Then, in 1
gal went from bad t
the Germans thre

At churches in Faro traditional values have not lost their importance. As in centuries past, work stops for solemn religious procession.

people in Lisbon. The epicentre of the quake is thought to have been just off the Algarve coast, possibly between Faro and Tavira. Witnesses claimed to have seen a fiery volcano erupt from beneath the sea just before the first jolt. A nightmarish tidal wave swept as far as 4 miles inland.

Throughout the Algarve, virtually every important monument—cathedral, castle or mansion—was destroyed or critically damaged. Among the hardest-hit towns was Lagos, which lost its castle, all its churches and the palace in which Henry the Navigator had lived. One tower, atop St.

Peter's church in
lously escaped
only to be knock
years later in a cy

Political Upheav
At the turn of t
tury political tr
throughout Eur
epicentre of Pari
Revolution worri
ities in Portugal.
radical books a
The situation
melancholy Port
Maria I, that sh
power to her s
Regent João. In
family fled to B
leon's soldiers i
gal.
First Spain,
gal, rose up agai
occupation in t
War. Among th
for independenc
lion in the Alg
Olhão. On June
townsfolk—arm
more than ar
spears and st
and captured th
son. Two days
Portuguese flag
flying above the
two young fishe
from Olhão in
They sailed all t
zil, carrying n

Reading the Map

Finding your way round in the Algarve is easy provided you've mastered a few essential words. Here's a list containing most of the words you're likely to come across during your explorations.

avenida	avenue
barragem	dam
Câmara Municipal	Town Hall
capela	chapel
casa	house
castelo	castle
cidade	town
claustro	cloister
convento	convent
cruz	cross
entrada	entrance
escada	stairs
fortaleza	fortress
igreja	church
largo	square
mercado	market
miradouro	belvedere, viewing point
mosteiro	monastery
paço, palácio	palace
parque	park
ponte	bridge
praça	square, plaza
praia	beach
rio	river
rua	street
Sé	Cathedral
saída	exit
torre	tower
túmulo	tomb
vista	view

What to See

Wherever your base in the Algarve, every pleasure and convenience is likely to be close at hand: beach and swimming pool, golf courses and shopping, restaurants and night life. But don't let the comfort deprive you of a better acquaintance with the country.

The easiest way of getting around is by car, but you can cover almost all the same ground by bus. Most of the towns are served by a railway line, too. Excursion firms run several different coach tours of the region—always the best way to get your bearings.

However you travel, you'll want to see a fair amount of the Algarve's varied terrain: the flat, beachy Sotavento coast; the cliffs and sandy coves of the western Barlavento sector; and the fertile highlands. But there's more to see than scenery; historic towns, distinctive architecture, the fishing industry, museums, famous or almost undiscovered resorts, ancient ruins.

We've divided the Algarve here into half a dozen zones suitable for one-day outings. We begin on the eastern extremity of the coast, the 30-mile stretch leading to the Spanish border.

Sotavento Coast

Heading east from the provincial capital of Faro (see p. 37), the first significant town is the proud fishing port of **Olhão.** You couldn't confuse this with any other place in the Algarve, for the architecture is more North African than Portuguese. Instead of the red tile roofs and filigreed chimneys seen elsewhere in the Algarve, Olhão's flat-topped houses are surmounted by terraces or belvederes called *açoteias.* Many houses have narrow outside staircases leading to additional whitewashed towers or lookouts—convenient for wives of fishermen, or smugglers.

Olhão's fishermen, some of whom sail off as far as Newfoundland to catch cod, have always been renowned for their fearlessness on the high seas. But in the last century or two, some sailors turned from fishing to the cargo trade between Portugal and North Africa. This relatively recent commercial link with the neighbouring continent is said to have been the inspiration for Olhão's casbah-style architecture. In any case, it developed long after the Moors had been ejected from the Algarve.

The high-point of local history came in 1808 when an im-

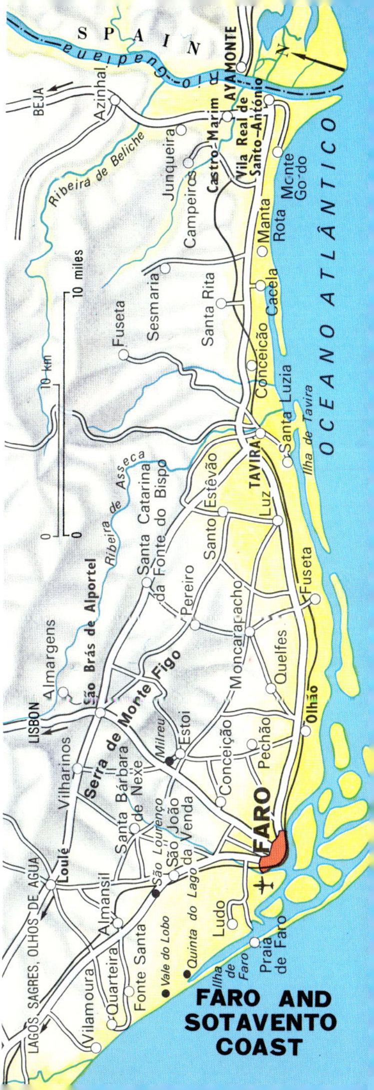

provised local army rebelled against Napoleon's occupation forces (see p. 22). This insurrectionary zeal led to the restoration of Portuguese rule throughout the country and Olhão won the title "Noble Town of the Restoration".

The **municipal market,** on the waterfront, occupies twin brick buildings as big as airplane hangars—one for fish and the other for everything else. A little farther on stands a well-tended park containing outsize roses and a compound for geese, ducks and black swans. Beyond the park is the pier from which ferryboats go to beaches on the islands just offshore. An earthy nightlife flourishes in this district, salty enough for any sailor.

Much of the coastline at this stage of the Sotavento is somewhat dreary. To make the most of the saline delta, salt pans have been dug in many places. As the summer heat leaves the basins full of pure white crystals, it's not quite the stuff of picture postcards but a relief from the expanses of tundra-like meadow.

Closer to Tavira, the countryside becomes more bountiful, with citrus and olive groves and vineyards. Tavira's grapes produce a hearty, rustic wine well known in the Algarve.

Surrounded by this prosperous agricultural area, **Tavira** is a spacious, self-assured town of churches and imposing buildings. Tavira may have been founded by Phoenicians or Carthaginians but the Romans left the most visible and practical monument: the foundation of their original seven-arch stone **bridge** is still in use, supporting the modern span across the River Gilão which divides the town. A plaque at the western edge of the bridge commemorates another historic fact. Here the "valorous residents of Tavira and Faro" repelled the forces of King Juan I of Castile, who was attempting a 14th-century invasion.

Just upstream you may see local women kneeling on the stones, scrubbing clothes in the river. Downstream is the fishing port. The boats you see here were among those which used to be involved in the so-called bullfights of the sea—the hunting and harpooning of great shoals of tunny fish. Economic considerations have ended that style of fishing.

The **town hall,** on the triangular plaza near the bridge, is

Workers rake salt crystals drying in hot sunshine of the Sotavento.

distinguished by its medieval arcades. Elsewhere, 17th- and 18th-century houses, some flaunting noble coats of arms, add to the aristocratic atmosphere. The skyline of domes and spires is dominated by the remains of a castle and a powerful red brick town wall. The **Igreja de Santa Maria do Castelo** (Church of St. Mary of the Castle), a national monument, was built on the ruins of a mosque soon after Tavira was reconquered from the Moors in 1242. The Gothic portal is the only part of the original still standing. Known as the City of Churches, or even more fancifully as the

From Net to Tin

Any night, on the ocean a mile or two beyond your beach, you may see eerie specks of light resembling an invasion fleet or a reconnaissance party from outer space. The lights are the lanterns of two or three dozen fishing boats in a wide formation, luring fish into an elaborate net structure.

For centuries fishing has been big business in the Algarve. But the boom began 100 years ago when the canning industry came to the region. Food distribution problems in two world wars added to the need for the harvest from the Algarve sea. To this day thousands of tons of fish are caught, tinned and exported annually. The most widely netted fish is the tunny (tuna). These fish are found in warm oceans of the world and have been known to grow up to 12 feet long and weigh over 1,000 lbs.

Algarvian Rome, Tavira once had six convents and still has more churches than most towns twice its size.

To the east of Tavira, the **beaches** develop ever more sumptuous dimensions, climaxing at **Monte Gordo.** This is a whopper of a beach by any standard, a deep band of golden sand separating the sea from the gradually sloping pine

Bountiful boats crowd the harbour; just back from a deep-sea expedition, Algarve trawlers are the backbone of the fishing industry.

forests of the interior. Monte Gordo's other claim to fame —actually *on* the beach—is its casino. Under one roof are all the facilities for elegant night-life and gambling.

The Guadiana river, which runs into the Atlantic about two miles east of Monte Gordo, has been a natural frontier for more than 2,000 years. In 27 B.C. the Romans chose the river to mark the boundary between the provinces of Lusitania and Baetica, which were to become Portugal and southern Spain. This explains the strategic importance of **Castro Marim,** a fortress-town rising from the flatlands to command

Sun-seeking vacationers flock to the open beach at Monte Gordo. But Algarve locals wear hats and hide in cafés to stay in the shade.

the broad river. You can walk the battlements for a defender's-eye view of the Spanish city of Ayamonte across the Guadiana, and stroll the castle grounds through the old Roman cemetery, waterworks and hospital. The ancient prison set the world standard for horrible hellholes.

Castro Marim is rich in history from several other eras. Excavations show that Bronze Age people took advantage of the security of the hilltop. The Phoenicians used it as a base in their travels up the river to mine copper and tin. In ancient times the estuary followed a different pattern, so the river came right up to the hillside; until the 17th century Castro Marim, now landlocked, was a fishing and cargo port.

For five centuries the primitive **castle-fortress** was occupied by the Moors. The Christian forces recaptured it in 1242 (according to one unglamorous version, without a fight).

The Portuguese soon began a campaign to populate Castro Marim for strategic reasons. And in 1319 it became the home of the new Military Order of Christ, which succeeded the disbanded Knights Templar. An inscription inside the castle's main entrance says that Henry the Navigator, who was a governor of the order, once lived within the fortress. No other relic of the prince is to be found on the premises, but he would have frequented the 14th-century **Igreja de Santiago** (Church of St. James) in the compound. Reduced to ruins in the great quake of 1755, the church has recently been the object of a reconstruction programme. The town became the Algarve's most important military base in the 17th century, with the development of a second fort, O Forte de S. Sebastião, on a hill across the way.

But there's more to Castro Marim than impressive walls and a tidy village. It's also exciting for bird-watchers. The unpolluted marshland of the **Castro Marim Nature Reserve** is controlled by the National Park Service. The aim is to protect the zone's botanical rarities, rich shellfish and bird life. Some migratory birds like the place so much they break the usual rules and stay all year round; like those sun-tanned human expatriates long resident in the Algarve, they see no reason to leave.

Just south of Castro Marim, **Vila Real de Santo António** is meant to be grandiose (in order to impress the Spanish just across the river). This is how a

Atop ancient Castro Marim castle, with 17th-century fort in background, local workman and mascot look across Guadiana river towards Spain.

military mind would design a town—all right-angles and parallel lines. Even the paving of the pedestrian precinct consists of rectangular designs instead of typically Portuguese mosaics. But in spite of its self-conscious air, Vila Real ("royal town") provides a pleasant show-window for the Algarve.

The rigid 18th-century town plan was the inspiration of the

Marquis of Pombal, the dynamic hatchet-man of King José I. Vila Real rose from nothing in five months of 1774, a crash building programme aimed at flexing economic if not military muscles at Spain. The **town square** *(Praça do Marques do Pombal)*, stately in distinguished simplicity, is surrounded on all four sides by two and three-storey buildings, with a white church slightly taller than the other structures. The plaza is paved in black and white stone in the form of wedges radiating from the centre in an unusual sunray effect; orange trees around the edges add colour and scent. The obelisk in the centre of the square has a gushing inscription dedicated to the king ("...most clement father of his vassals, protector of innocence, supreme avenger of oppression..."). Today, despite its martial history, Vila Real is not exactly bristling with arms; a couple of Portuguese patrol boats, smaller than trawlers, might be nosing around the fishing port but otherwise all's peaceful.

Since the Spanish town of Ayamonte is only 15 minutes away by ferryboat, a certain cosmopolitan atmosphere is superimposed on the provincial life of Vila Real. Spaniards often come over for sightseeing and shopping, especially for the commodities which are currently cheaper in Portugal. Escudos and pesetas are interchangeable in shops. The frontier is open from 8 a.m. to 8 p.m. in winter and until 11 p.m. in summer; ferryboats leave from each side at least every half hour.

Ayamonte, in the Spanish province of Huelva, is bigger than Vila Real. The *ayuntamiento* (town hall) has a classic patio with palm trees, a fountain, arches and tiled walls—all open to the sky. Facing the municipal building, a small park fenced in by 24 tall palms is decorated with illustrated coloured tiles, as if to show the Portuguese they have no mo-

Waiting for something to happen, local lads stake out the main square of model frontier town, Vila Real, surrounded by bitter orange trees.

nopoly on *azulejos* (spelled the same in both languages but pronounced somewhat differently: AZOO-LAI-JOOSH in Portuguese, ATHOO-LAI-GHOS in Spanish).

From the government-run *parador* (inn) on a high bluff above Ayamonte you get an eye-filling **view** of the white Spanish town below, the wide meandering Guadiana river, and, across the way, Portugal, looking curiously flat.

At the ferryboat landing a souvenir shop does a lively trade in last-minute Spanish souvenirs—guitars, bullfight swords, toy bulls, leather hats and collapsible fans.

Faro and Uplands

The provincial capital of the Algarve has a certain charm. **Faro** (population estimated as high as 50,000) has greatly expanded, both horizontally and vertically, though many streets still consist of white-washed single-storey houses guarded by dogs napping in the dust. The tempo is relaxed in this administrative outpost far from Lisbon's pressures.

Most of the tourists who fly in to Faro airport go directly to their resorts up and down the shore. But they return to look at Faro's historic sights and shop in the "big city" stores. Here, as in several other Algarve towns, the main shopping street is reserved for pedestrians. In other ways, too, the centre of Faro is pleasant: a cobbled, shaded municipal garden with an open-air café and an old-fashioned bandstand; a small-boat harbour; and a charming old walled city-within-the-city.

The main entrance to the old town is the 18th-century **Arco da Vila,** alongside the munic-

Pedestrians rule: plaza in Spanish town of Ayamonte (left) and main street of Algarve's capital, Faro.

ipal tourist office at the south end of the garden. The curves and angles of the arch and its setting are repeated high above in the bell tower, on top of which a venerable family of storks maintains its nest.

Recent archaeological research seems to confirm that Faro was the site of a big Roman city called Ossonoba, important enough to coin its own money. During the centuries of Arab domination it thrived. One of the ruling families was named Harune, from which the name of Faro may derive.

The Christian troops of King Afonso III recaptured and redeveloped the town in 1249. But most monuments were destroyed in 1596 when Faro, then under the flag of Spain, was sacked by a British expeditionary force. Whatever was left came tumbling down later in the earthquake of 1755.

Until comparatively recent times, when the area silted into a tidal flat, Faro was a fishing and commercial port open to the Atlantic. The British fleet of 1596 sailed straight up to the city walls. Nowadays small fishing boats and pleasure craft have to zigzag carefully amidst the dunes, and then creep beneath the railway bridge to enter the sleepy harbour.

In the same building as the harbour master's office, a small maritime **museum** *(Museu Marítimo)* displays items of nautical nostalgia: old navigational instruments, lanterns, models of historic sailing ships. Concise exhibits also show how to build a boat, tie a knot and lay a fishnet. The walls are covered with paintings of the fish you might catch.

The first layer of the city walls is said to have been built in neolithic times, then amplified by the Moors and rebuilt and expanded after the reconquest. Within them the old town of Faro makes an agreeable stroll. But on a hot afternoon, when the cobbles of the wide open **Largo da Sé** (cathedral square) are broiling, you'll appreciate the cool hideaway of the **Sé** (cathedral). It was built in the second half of the 13th century, right after the expulsion of the Moors, probably on the ruins of a mosque. Of the original Gothic building only the main portico and tower remain. Inside, the dimensions are unexpectedly square. The decorations run to all the cherubs that could be carved, plus some fine *azulejos.*

A monument of 16th-century Portugal, the **Convento de Nossa Senhora da Assunção** (Convent of Our Lady of the

FARO-CENTRE
OCEANO ATLÂNTICO
Doca de Recreio
PORTIMÃO, SAGRES
LISBON
ESTAÇÃO C. FERRO
VILA REAL DE S. ANTÓNIO, SPAIN
N
Igreja do Carmo
Largo do Carmo
Correios
Museu Marítimo
Museu Etnográfico Regional
Museu Arqueológico
Tourist Office
Arco da Vila
Sé
Largo da Sé
Praça Afonso III
São Francisco
Largo de São Francisco
Largo do Castelo
Jardim Manuel Bivar
Praça D. Francisco Gomes
Praça Ferreira Almeida
Praça A. Herculano
Largo de São Pedro
Largo Silva Porto
Largo das Mouras Velhas
Largo Sol
Largo 25 Abril
Largo Mota
Rua General Teófilo Trindade
Rua Infante Dom Henrique
Rua Serpa Pinto
R. da Boavista
Rua V. Coelho
Rua F. Barreto
R. Teófilo Braga
Rua Baptista Pinto
Rua da Madalena
Rua de São Pedro
Rua Filipe Alistão
Rua José Estêvão
Rua do Compromisso
Rua do Prior
Trv. José Coelho
Trv. dos Arcos
Rua Conselheiro Bivar
Rua Gil Eanes
Rua do Forno
Rua da Cruz
Rua da Barqueta
Avenida da República
Rua 1° de Maio
Rua da Marinha
Rua Ivens
Rua D. F. Gomes
Rua do Alportel
R. F. Neto
R.C. Melo
Rua Barreto
R.G. Brito
Rua Sotto Mayor
Cabreira
Rua Horta Machado
R. João de Deus
Rua da Cruz das Mestras
Rua F. Horta
Rua Cúmano
Rua Dr. Justino
A. Garrett
Rua do Sol
Rua Baptista Lopes
Rua Letes
Rua de Portugal
Rua Dr. J. Lúcio
Rua Vasco da Gama
Rua de Santo António
Rua 1° de Dezembro
Rua Rebelo da Silva
Rua A. Castilho
R. A. Castilho
Rua João Dias
Rua M. Belmarço
Rua A. Herculano
R.B. de Almeida
R. V. Almeida
Rua da Misericórdia
Rua do Albergue
Rua do Município
Rua D. Gueiro
Rua Rasquinho
R. Repouso
Rua Brandeiro
R.J.M.
Rua S. Francisco
Rua do Bocage
R. Reis Damazo
Rua Caçadores 4
R. D. Teresa Ramalho Ortigão
R. L. Cortes
Rua Dr. P. Sousa
Rua do Castelo
Rua Com. F. Manuel
0 600 1200 m
0 600 1200 yards

Statues, staircases, balustrades, gateways: 18th-century architecture at its best in Estoi palace.

Assumption) contains what's considered the most beautiful cloister in the Algarve. It also boasts the region's biggest chimney—not at all in the style of the delicate filigreed models seen on most houses. The convent was abandoned in the 19th century, then put to use as a cork factory. In recent times it has been reconstructed and turned into a valuable archaeological museum, **the Museu Arqueológico e Lapidar Infante D. Henrique.**

The great attraction of this museum is 2,000 years old: a Roman **mosaic** unearthed in a house in Faro's Rua D. Henrique during the construction of a sewer line. This beautiful work, 30 feet long and 10 feet wide, has been put back together in a room of its own in the museum. In the centre of the mosaic is the portrait of a handsome bearded god of the sea with worried eyes; unfortunately the bulldozer that discovered the mosaic in 1976 shaved off the lower half of his face.

Elsewhere in the museum you can see pre-Roman and Roman inscriptions, fossils and prehistoric tools. One large hall holds an art collection bequeathed by a local diplomat, Ferreida de Almeida. Many of the paintings are devoted to the first world war, nudes, and the collector himself (13 of his portraits in all).

Another museum within easy walking distance, the **Museu Etnográfico Regional** (Regional Ethnographic Museum), contains a simulated village street. Rooms of typical Algarve houses are authentically furnished, and life-like dummies "model" rustic costumes. A handicrafts display includes many wickerwork inventions and some inspired designs for chimneys. One exhibit is the actual water cart which Manuel Ignacio Miguel of Olhão operated for 60 years, almost to his death in 1974. He travelled the region selling fresh water in huge pottery jars, until the modern supply network put him and his donkey out of business.

Among Faro's many churches, big and small, the **Igreja do Carmo** (Carmelite Church) is usually described as the most beautiful. Its twin baroque towers rise above an artfully balanced façade on the square where you'll also find the main post office. The church's interior is richly decorated with 18th-century carvings. For the strong-nerved, a **Capela dos Ossos** (chapel of bones) may be reached through a side entrance. This 19th-century vault employed the skulls and bones of parishioners as construction material instead of brick or stone. One volume listing the monuments of the Algarve suggests that this may be the most notable bone chapel in the entire country.

For some light relief you can drive or take a bus out to PRAIA DE FARO, the long sweep of sandy beach out past the airport. A single-lane causeway links the Praia's dunes with the mainland. Or go by ferry from a pier alongside the old town wall. If the ocean is rough you can swim on the opposite side of the long spit of sand, in the calmer waters of the inland sea.

In the pleasant agricultural zone inland from Faro, the village of **Estoi** has two historical sites. A short walk down a shaded avenue from the village church, the sadly neglected 18th-century **palace** of Estoi is set amidst formal gardens. The decorations, changed over the years, show different tastes: busts of historic characters are impaled on the parapets, and some walls are devoted to tile panels of voluptuous nudes.

Just down the road from the centre of the village are the remains of a palace built 1,400 years before the palace of Estoi. The **ruins of Milreu** were originally thought to have been the site of the city of Ossonoba. But Faro itself now claims that distinction, and Milreu is considered to be merely the very large country house of an eminent figure of the Roman empire, identity unknown. The outline of this luxury establishment, which follows a gradual

Milreu mosaic hints that Romans admired Algarve fish; housewives buy today's catch in plastic bags.

slope, is clear to see. A sunken bath, with mosaic fish designs, is reasonably well preserved. It was a private bath, and not for the supernumeraries or slaves.

But the sight that excites historians most is the tall semicircular walls, still standing, of a **temple** consecrated to pagan water gods. It appears that

even as late as the 4th century A.D. the proprietor of the palace was still resisting Christianity. Archaeologists are tantalized to imagine the treasures which must have been looted from Milreu before anyone thought of protecting them, in the 18th century.

A quick way to refresh the spirit after too much sun and beach is to ride up through fertile farm country to **São Brás de Alportel.** Almond, carob and olive trees are the most obvious source of wealth here. The town itself is clean and roomy with many of the typical Algarvian chimneys to enhance the skyline. Beyond the town, at the top of a considerable hill, is a government-sponsored *pousada* (inn). The **view** from the terrace of the *pousada* extends over rich green fields and orchards, the orange tile roofs of São Brás, and in fact most of the central Algarve. Flower gardens surround the inn with roses, geraniums, honeysuckle and sunflowers, among other attractions.

Local historians recall the year 1596 with pride. After the British sacked Faro, they advanced on São Brás. Defiant, although unarmed except for sticks and clubs, the citizens came out to meet the foe. Their cave-man style of counter-attack scared away the invaders, and the natives of São Brás won the nickname of *cachamorreiros* (cudgel-wielders).

From São Brás the flower-lined road to Loulé passes through rolling orchards of fig, olive and orange trees. **Loulé,** a prosperous market town, has medieval **castle walls** and a parish church with a distinguished Gothic interior. An ambitious modern boulevard, shaded by sizeable trees and paved in mosaic designs, climbs from the centre of town. The market, housed in a curious structure of imitation Moorish architecture, offers fruit, fish and handicrafts.

In the back streets around the market the smell of leather, the sound of drills, sanders and hammers tell you artisans are at work. You can watch them producing furniture, copper bowls and brightly decorated saddles and bridles. The craftsmen of Loulé are said to be descendants of a community of Moslems who found refuge in the district after the Christian reconquest in the mid-13th century. Every springtime Loulé becomes the centre of life in the Algarve; the local Carnival, with parades, music and an unrestrained Battle of Flowers, attracts crowds of tourists and Algarvians.

West from Faro

The terrain gradually changes to the west of Faro as the long, flat coastline of the Sotavento begins to give way to the rugged, rocky terrain of the Barlavento. You wouldn't know it from the main highway or the railway line, as they parallel the shore several miles inland, mostly out of sight of the sea.

A few miles west of Faro a simple white church stands out upon a small hill overlooking the main road. The road sign says "S. Lourenço" (St. Lawrence). You've never seen anything quite like the blue and white interior of the **São Lourenço** church. Almost every square inch of the walls and vaulted ceilings is covered with 250-year-old *azulejos* of biblical scenes. The only exception to the colour scheme is the gilt-carved altar.

São Lourenço's beautiful

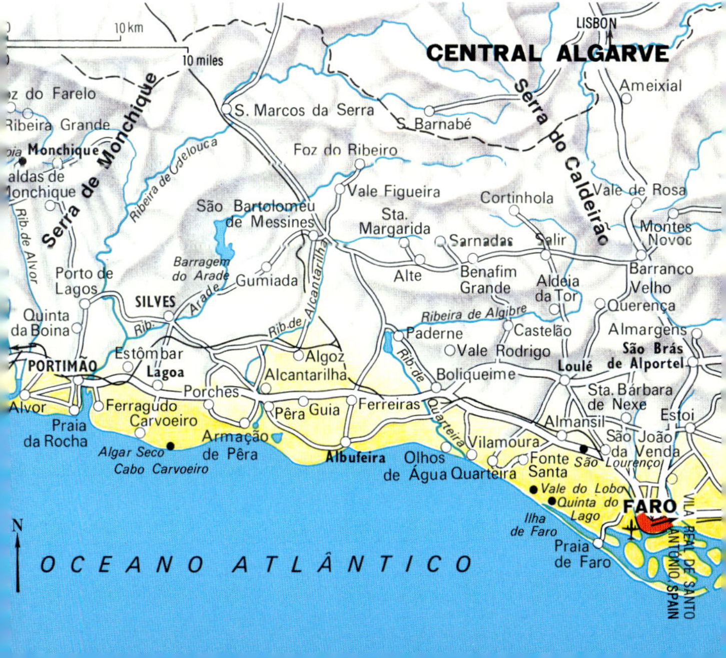

Manueline Innovations

During the reign of Manuel I (1495–1521), artists were inspired as never before by the discovery of far-away lands and the excitement of long sea voyages. The style they evolved, called "Manueline" after the monarch, celebrated travel and the sea.

Motifs like anchors, knotted rope, sails, terrestrial globes, marine plants and animals, corn cobs and laurel leaves, pearls and coral were the inventive commonplace of sculpture and architecture. Furniture was inlaid with exotic marquetry, mother-of-pearl and ivory, showing the strong influence of India and the Orient.

Masters of the Manueline style include the architect Boytac, renowned for his twisted columns, the Arruda brothers, who gave Moorish touches to their buildings and the painters Vasco Fernandes, Gaspar Vaz and Jorge Afonso.

Although the most famous work of Manueline art is considered to be Lisbon's Belém Tower, there are some examples of the style in the Algarve. They make a rich contrast with the massive severity of the Gothic and the classic simplicity of the Renaissance and are instantly recognizable.

country church comes under the jurisdiction of the town of ALMANSIL, a regional shopping centre. So does **Quinta do Lago,** an expensive urbanization occupying 2,000 acres of pine hills. With its own golf course, riding academy, tennis courts and salt lake, this development calls itself the lowest-density leisure-living area in Europe. The limited number of luxury villas are discreetly tucked away.

Vale do Lobo (valley of the wolf), an expensive "touristic village" to the west, has a five-star hotel, plus villas and apartments. Among the many built-in recreational facilities is a golf course from where there are splendid views over the Atlantic. It's also an excellent tennis centre.

Quarteira, a booming resort town, has come a long way from the original fishing village of that name. The apartment blocks and hotels now stretch so far from the centre that a horsecarriage taxi service operates along the front. In the old town, the low-rise fishermen's quarter, the municipal

Rhapsody in blue and gold: elegant church in hamlet of São Lourenço.

market is right on the beach; shoppers have been known to arrive in bikinis. The fish auction shed is the scene of exciting bidding and chatter when the catch comes in. Between the auction and the market is a major concession to the tourist invasion—a wickerwork mart selling everything you ever imagined could be made of straw, and then a few more inventions.

Quarteira's beach is long enough for all the fishing boats plus all the tourists, Portuguese and foreign. Every couple of hundred yards the strand is divided by a stone breakwater, giving each segment a separate identity and saving the sand from the erosion of the constant washing of the waves.

While Quarteira just grew like a vine, its westerly neighbour, **Vilamoura,** was planned down to the last snack bar, tennis court and fire hydrant. Vilamoura is called Europe's biggest private tourist undertaking, a 4,000-acre entreprise which will eventually house 55,000 people. Hotels, villas and apartments are scattered amidst two golf courses (two more are planned), the Algarve's biggest water-sport centre, and a farm producing fruit, vegetables, wine and milk. To complete the facilities, a casino has been opened and operates on the premises.

Building the 615-boat **marina** was an immense project but not totally original. The Romans had built an artificial harbour in very nearly the same place. An important fishing, fish-salting and shipping operation was centred here in Roman times.

The remains of **Cêrro da Vila,** as the site is called, were unearthed just across the road from the new Vilamoura marina. It was inhabited for eight centuries by Romans, Visigoths and finally Moors, and each society left its mark. After you've looked over the foundations of the buildings, the elaborate water piping system and

Fisherman (left) shares his beach with vacationers at Olhos de Agua. Below: yachts from several seas convene at Vilamoura's luxury port.

the surviving mosaics, you can visit the small museum on the spot. Everything in it has been recovered from Cêrro da Vila; fishhooks and coins, vases and chunks of marble statues.

Westward from Vilamoura the coastline begins to show the rock formations which make the Barlavento area so fascinating. There are said to be 82 beaches *with names* on the Algarve, not to mention hidden coves. One of the most unusual, between Vilamoura and the big resort of Albufeira, is **Olhos de Agua.** An intimate beach, harbouring a small fleet of fishing boats, is surrounded on three sides by pine cliffs. Intriguing rock shapes rise from the sea, and in one of the coves fresh water flows from rocks which are visible only at low tide.

Albufeira, once a picturesque fishermen's town, is alas now vastly overexploited. Its pockmarked sandstone cliffs rim a roomy beach lined up with colourful fishing boats. On a sunny summer day, the tractor hauling the boats onto the sand has to manœuvre amongst sunbathers in bikinis and impromptu soccer games. Even before the boat is fully ashore, tourists, fishwives and off-duty fishermen gather to gape at the catch. The main beach is linked to the centre of the town by a tunnel cut down through the cliff.

Weird rock formations are typical of Barlavento coast, as at Albufeira.

Starting near the main plaza, an open-air market goes endlessly on through the streets. The variety of goods on sale reaches its peak on Sunday: home-made cheeses, live chickens and ducks, herbs and spices, and mouth-watering fruits and vegetables from nearby farms. Also embroidery, home-made sweets, rabbits and puppies, hand-carved back-scratchers and last year's fashions.

Albufeira's **cliff-top** position and labyrinthine street layout had a military significance in the mid-13th century. Entrenched in this easily defensible spot, the Moors were able to hold out against the main drive by King Afonso III to expel them from Portugal. Albufeira was one of the last towns to fall.

In Largo Jacinto d'Ayet a bold modern **statue** honours a native son of Albufeira, Vicente de Carvalho. An Augustinian friar, he was arrested during a period when Christians were being persecuted in Japan in 1632. The statue portrays his martyrdom at Nagasaki—he was burned at the stake. (Father Vincent was beatified in 1867.)

Albufeira is well supplied with shops, bars and restaurants. It's easy to explore on foot, but its slippery cobbled streets go up, down and around unpredictably, so it's possible to lose your way. But wherever you are in the maze of striking white houses; you're never far from the Atlantic. From almost any vantage point, the views of Albufeira and its seascape are spectacular.

Filigreed Flues

Tourism is sometimes called the industry without chimneys. In the Algarve that's not wholly accurate.

Chimneys are an indispensable part of the attractions of the region. For hundreds of years the owners of Algarve houses have taken pride in the beauty and originality of their latticed chimneys. Originally they were carved from tree-trunks, later in ceramic. Less romantically, cement is usual today, and you may see two chimneys alike, but not often. The graceful, ornamented chimney-towers are still the pride of the Algarve skyline.

Silves to the Summit

Once upon a time, more than eight centuries ago, **Silves** was a magnificent city of palaces, gardens and bazaars. Sailing ships carried the treasures of the east up the busy Arade river from the Atlantic. Today, the silted river is only a sluggish shadow of what it once was. Gypsies bathe among a few weary rowing boats and the town is a backwater, as evocative as a rusted old treasure chest.

But while the riches of Silves were stolen long ago, the looters couldn't take the priceless setting. The white town climbs the hillside from the river to a vast castle, the whole surrounded by mile after mile of orchards—oranges, lemons, grapefruit, clementines and pomegranates.

The era of good fortune for Silves began with the Moslem invasion in A.D. 711. The occupying forces made Silves, called Chelb, the capital of the Algarve. With comprehensive fortifications and a population in the tens of thousands, Chelb was considered one of the strongest outposts in 12th-century Arab Iberia.

In 1189, an international brigade of Portuguese troops and Crusaders besieged, captured and sacked Silves. The Moors recaptured it in 1191. Six years later the Christians attacked again but were repulsed and the final conquest was delayed until 1249. Yet the nadir was still to come. In the late 16th century, the bishopric of the Algarve was transferred to Faro, leaving Silves with a population of 140 men, women and children... and memories.

Silves had a castle long before the invasion from North Africa. Even before the Carthaginians, historians say, there had been a fort on the hill. The Romans conquered it in 201 B.C., and later Moorish modifications must have been impressive. After the reconquest the lines of the present **fortress**—much restored in modern times—took form.

The inside of the castle is less warlike than you'd think. Oleander and jacaranda soften the mood, and the view from the walls and turrets down upon the tile roofs of the town and the surrounding citrus groves is delightful.

The **Sé** (Cathedral) of Silves was built in the 13th century, presumably on the site of an important mosque. Vandalism, earthquakes and time itself have severely damaged the big, old Gothic church, but it has recently been much restored. Though it lost its rank when the bishop moved out 400 years ago, the cathedral retains a majestic air.

Down along the riverfront an airy white structure about the size and shape of a modest cathedral serves as the town's fruit, vegetable and fish market. Once a month, the fairground nearby is filled with echoes of the Arab past—a hubbub of commerce under a great expanse of canvas. You can buy a belt or a basket, a hammer or a sickle, pots and pans, or a pig or a cow. City-bred tourists will enjoy mingling with the region's livestock, watching the shrewd buying and selling procedures. Visiting experts can compare notes on milk yield or sheep-shearing. In the side-streets around the market you can still find stables. You may even happen upon a donkey having its mane clipped.

On the road (N 124) leading from town to the north-east stands a small but much admired monument. The **Cross of Portugal** is a 16th-century symbol of the Christian reconquest of the Algarve from the Moslems. Carved from a 10-foot tall piece of limestone, it shows Christ crucified on one face, and descended from the cross on the reverse. From this point there is a good view up to Silves castle.

Continuing along the north-eastern road, the highway cuts through stony hill country planted with olive and almond trees. It's well worth stopping in the village of **Alte,** and not just because the name may derive from the order, *"Alto!"* (halt). Legend says a noble-woman of the district, on a long, exhausting pilgrimage to the nearest town with a church, halted her convoy here and ordered the establishment of a settlement—with a more convenient church. The present country-style church in the centre of Alte dates from the 16th century. Inside, blue-and-white painted tiles from the 18th century depict biblical events.

A "welcome" plaque in five languages at the entrance to Alte is your first clue that it's

Water must still be hand-carried in picturesque hill village of Alte.

A cool drink after a hard day's work; tile roofs of Monchique.

special. In fact, Alte is a carefully preserved, thoroughly inviting village of freshly whitewashed houses with bright, original adornments—shrubs, flowers or painted colour schemes. Though the character of Alte is uniform, no two houses are entirely alike. A brook descending to and through the town waters a rich, narrow valley thick with orange, pomegranate and fig trees.

Another highland highlight (off the road between Silves and Alte) is the **Barragem do Arade** (Arade dam), a refreshing change from seascapes. The water collected in this reservoir surrounded by pine hills makes possible the irrigation of the area's profitable orchards and it's a pleasant picnic spot. The overbearing stone column erected in dedication of the dam is engraved with a long quotation signed "Salazar", the late dictator—an irresistible target for graffiti.

On the way from Silves to the highest point of the Algarve, pause at **Caldas de Monchique,** a spa which has been known since Roman times for its therapeutic waters. Quaffing the local water, fresh from the springs, is supposed to make anyone feel ten years younger—once you get past the sulphurous aroma. The 15th-century Portuguese king João II was a great fan of Monchique water. In Edwardian times the spa was considered a most fashionable place to restore health and vigour. Today, the sleepy hollow of Caldas de Monchique is pervaded by nostalgia. Uphill from the spa, alongside a rushing stream, picnic tables are arrayed in the shade of giant eucalyptus trees.

If you can't make it to the spa, all is not lost: you can consume the same water, carbonated or still, by the bottle in any bar or restaurant in the Algarve. An efficient bottling plant has transformed the formerly elite practice of "taking the waters" at Caldas de Monchique into a big business.

Northward from Caldas the road weaves uphill past terraced farmlands and forests of

chestnut, oak and cork. The market town of **Monchique** is a centre of handicrafts: you can buy home-made nougat, the tasty distilled spirit called *medronho* made from the fruit of the arbutus tree, hand-carved wooden utensils or a straw bag big enough for carrying a pig.

One of the steep cobbled streets climbing from the little main square leads to the sparkling white **parish church** of Monchique. The main portal is

Livestock traders gather monthly on a Monchique hillside. Opposite: looking down on bathers and boats.

distinctively carved of stone in the Manueline style. Inside, it's also a typically Portuguese sort of church with three naves, a wooden ceiling, parquet floor and glazed painted tiles lining the bottom of the walls. High above the town the ruins of a 17th-century convent loom like a grey eminence.

Once a month on a shaded hillside above the marketplace of Monchique, the area's farmers gather with their sheep and goats, cows and pigs for a lively trading session. It's a colourful country scene with a background sound of excited barnyard noises.

A few miles beyond Monchique, above the eucalyptus, pine and mimosa, **Foia** is the end of the line, the summit, almost 3,000 feet above sea level. A chunky obelisk marks the highest point in the Algarve. The brisk smell of mountain herbs and flowers is a big change from the African-style parched heat of the coastal plain. From the rocky lookout area you get a splendid **panorama** from Portimão Bay to the Sagres peninsula. At Foia, as in other beauty spots, vendors lie in wait for the tourist coaches.

West from Albufeira

The beach of **Armação de Pêra** is so long that it seems to straddle both halves of the Algarve coastline. For several miles to the east, it's one vast golden dune. But at the western end, the terrain changes into a series of rocky coves. The recent tourist development—hotels, apartment blocks and villas—has eclipsed the original fishing village. But everyone gets along together. The swimming beach and the fishermen's beach meet and informally overlap, depending on the needs of the visitors or the permanent residents.

On the oceanfront in the centre of town, a small fortress built in 1760 contains a pretty little chapel. A mile or two to the west, on a promontory boldly jutting into the sea, stands a small white chapel with a pyramidal steeple. The chapel of **Nossa Senhora da Rocha** (Our Lady of the Rock) is a real fishermen's church. Aside from religious images the simple 17th-century temple contains a model of a caravelle and a painting of a sailing ship foundering in a storm. Each side of the promontory looks on to a small beach; actually the two coves are connected by a tunnel through the rock.

Lagoa, a relaxed inland town with a stately church, is best known for its wine. Travellers who stop here long enough to stroll the old streets soon note the heady aroma of ageing wine seeping from the local *adegas* (wine cellars). Lagoa is the province's wine capital. The *vinho da casa* served in most Algarve restaurants comes from here. (Lagoa wine, both red and white, is more powerful than ordinary wine; the extra degree or two of alcoholic content can creep up and surprise you.) Lagoa is also important as an agricultural market town, and a centre for handicrafts production. (Don't confuse Lagoa, pronounced lah-GO-ah, with the historic port town of Lagos, pronounced LAH-goosh, about 12 miles to the west.)

From Lagoa head south for the charming coastal resort of **Carvoeiro.** The beach is little more than a postage stamp compared with the expanse farther east, but Carvoeiro is the essence of the Barlavento coast: dramatic **cliffs** on which white houses perch, a crescent of sand, and a dozen fishing boats beached among the tents and parasols. Cafés and restaurants conveniently fill the background.

A road follows the cliffs east of Carvoeiro to the geological wonder of **Algar Seco** (literally, dry gully). Nature has made a double-deck arch of stone here, the upper level providing a walkway through the cliffside to a narrow balcony over the sea; below this is an arch through which the ocean flows, or crashes, in. The lagoon enclosed among these menacing cliffs—really an open-air grotto—is a snorkeller's delight.

Portimão is a big, professional fishing port at the mouth of the Arade river. You get a wide-angle view of the **harbour** chock-a-block with trawlers and auxiliary boats, plus a few yachts and dinghies, from the long bridge across the estuary on the way into town. Since this narrow causeway on the main east-west Algarve highway is easily jammed, you may have a longer look than you anticipated.

The hectic operations of the fishing industry are an engrossing tourist attraction in Portimão. You'll share the excitement as you stand on the wharf watching the "bucket brigade" hurling wickerwork baskets of fresh fish from deep in the hold all the way up to the ice-trays

Transparent water at Algar Seco intrigues snorkelling enthusiasts.

ashore. Full and empty baskets cross in the air almost automatically, with astonishing precision and speed. A siren growls to announce the start of one of the big-time fish auctions. Between rushes the fishermen squat along the wharf untangling their nets.

Portimão may have been one of the important cities of the ancient world. Some histories say it was founded by the Carthaginian general Hamilcar Barca, and was named Portus Annibalis in honour of his son, Hannibal. The Moors, who took the town from the Visigoths in the 8th century, changed the name to Porcimunt. This is apparently the basis for the Portuguese name Portimão.

As one of the Algarve towns which suffered the most during the earthquake of 1755, Portimão can offer the visitor almost no buildings or monuments of great historic interest. Perhaps to compensate for this, the town fathers have supplied the Largo 1º de Dezembro, the park opposite the tourist office, with benches of blue-and-white glazed tiles illustrating ten pivotal events in the history of Portugal. (The park's name comes from the date, December 1, 1640, when Portugal's independence from Spain was restored.)

Inland from the port and riverfront gardens Portimão has many cheerful streets in which tall new buildings coexist unusually well with the

A good catch: baskets of fish whiz through the air at Portimão.

small old houses around them.

A short ride by bus or donkey-cart *(carrinha)* from the centre of Portimão, beside the mouth of the Arade river, brings you to the most celebrated beach of the Algarve, **Praia da Rocha.** This immense, extravagantly sandy beach is framed by cliffs and rock formations. Walkways protect naked feet from the long sizzling stretches of open sand between the cliff face and the waterline. The vastness of Praia da Rocha ("beach of the rock") is recent; when the entry to Portimão harbour was dredged, a long jetty was built to protect it, and the excess

Village girl passes time with traditional needlework in progress.

sand was delivered to Praia da Rocha. At the end of the jetty, which seems a long way out to sea, anglers find plenty of fish waiting to bite.

Praia da Rocha is a major family resort with grand old villas and brand new hotels along with many more economical facilities. One of the Algarve's pioneer tourist hotels opened on its own sea-cliff at Praia da Rocha in 1934. The rooms of the Bela Vista, formerly a private palace, are decorated with 17th-, 18th- and 19th- century *azulejos.*

High above the beach and the mouth of the river, the 16th-century **Fortaleza de Sta. Catarina** (St. Catherine Fortress) looks fierce and inhospitable from the outside. But once you pass through the portal, you find the parade ground has been converted into a flower-decked patio well supplied with café tables and parasols.

Beyond Praia da Rocha are several interesting beaches, each with its own character. The sand of PRAIA DO VAU is said to be healthfully laced with iodine. The huge white sand beach of Alvor is the focus of a recreational area which includes a golf course and a casino. In the town of **Alvor,** the 16th-century parish church has a much-admired portico, carved in the flamboyant Manueline style. Though the evidence is vague, it's thought that Alvor may have been founded in 436 B.C. In modern times Alvor made history as the venue for the negotiations which brought about independence for the former Portuguese territory of Angola.

To World's End

Lagos, a peaceful yet lively town, has a rich historical past and an enterprising present. It's big enough to boast a bold boulevard and varied shopping and entertainment possibilities, but small enough that donkey carts can bottle up the traffic.

Lacobriga was the ancient Roman name for the town. Parts of the original Roman wall still stand, much expanded and rebuilt over the centuries and now restored—perhaps too perfectly to be true. But in the 8th century the defence line was no barrier to the great Moslem invasion. The Moors made the town an important trading port. During the reconquest of Portugal Lagos was much fought over.

Once under Portuguese sovereignty Lagos prospered. It was proclaimed the capital of the Algarve. The governor's palace was the headquarters for Henry the Navigator. A **statue** of the prince, seated with a sextant in hand and looking farsightedly across the harbour, has been erected on a plaza tesselated with a design of the waves. Arguments persist over the exact whereabouts of Henry's "School of Navigation", but it seems almost cer-

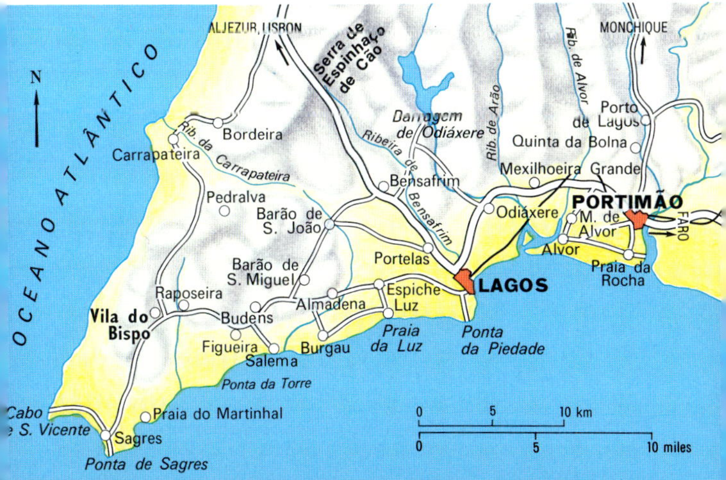

WESTERN ALGARVE AND SAGRES PENINSULA

tain that Lagos was the principal shipyard and port serving his team of explorers.

An early consequence of the explorations along the west coast of Africa in the middle of the 15th century was the establishment of the slave trade. Lagos became the key port in this commerce (finally abolished in the second half of the 19th century). You can see the place where Portugal's first slave auctions took place—in the small unmarked **arcade** in the corner of a white two-storey building at the north-east side of what is now Praça Infante D. Henrique (Henry the Navigator's Square). Most of the other historic buildings, and presumably the relics and papers of Prince Henry, were lost in the devastating earthquake of 1755.

One survivor of the golden age is the **altar** of the Chapel of St. Anthony, an exuberant little masterpiece in carved wood. This chapel, in the **Igreja de Santo António,** is rather overpowered by all the late baroque ideas in gilt; sculptured warriors and cherubs support columns of angels. The lower parts of the walls are covered with 18th-century tiles. A place of honour set in the floor goes to the tomb of an Irishman, Hugh Beaty, a technical adviser who commanded the Lagos regiment of the Portuguese army in the late 18th century.

Next door to the church, the **Museu Regional de Lagos** contains unusual ancient relics as well as items of folk and religious art. There are Roman mosaics unearthed in the district, at Abicada and Budens. You can read the original charter of Lagos issued in 1504, and admire the key to the city, evidently of the same epoch, in a chest as big as a shoe-box. The work of local artists and artisans includes clever farm implements and colourful donkey halters. The tiny mirrors which decorate them also reflect light, a prudent safety precaution for travelling the road at night. The section devoted to religious art features vestments worn at a mass in 1578 celebrated by order of King Sebastian shortly before his army departed for North Africa. There the charismatic 24-year-old king and his followers were wiped out in Portugal's worst military fiasco.

In the busiest part of town, the Portas de Portugal, a mod-

Glorious Baroque wooden carvings cover St. Anthony Chapel walls.

ern statue of Sebastian stirs controversy. Portrayed with heavy knight's gauntlets and helmet at the ready, he looks more like a mod motorcycle rider than a doomed king.

Just beyond Lagos the coastline becomes poetically rugged; tiny coves interspersed with weird rock formations. The most intriguing is **Ponta da Piedade** (Point of Piety) which is a truly unforgettable sea-cliff ensemble. On a calm day you can look all the way down at a perfectly transparent sea washing the dramatic rock bridges and grottoes. Very long stairways have been cut into the cliffside all the way down to sea level. The lighthouse has its own stand of palm trees.

The area around Lagos has other natural surprises. Irrigation from the Bravura dam makes the cultivation of rice possible. The flooded paddies give the countryside a brilliant splash of green, especially startling if you arrive in late summer when most of the farms are drab and dry. From Lagos toward the western extremity of the peninsula, fig trees hug the ground to escape the sea wind, which tousles the wheatfields and turns the windmills. Along the road are limestone kilns to keep the Algarve supplied with whitewash; tradition

rules that houses have to be painted twice a year.

Because the Sagres peninsula takes the brunt of the Atlantic winds and tides, the beaches even this far west are remarkably roomy and sandy. Between an awesome headland and a charming white fishing village, PRAIA DA LUZ is well established as a family resort. Westward, still in the lee of Sagres point, the beaches of BURGAU and SALEMA are welcoming holiday spots.

At **Sagres** itself, the local fishing fleet, bobbing at anchor beneath a cliff, looks distressingly vulnerable. And in the village the one- and two-storey houses seem to crouch against the ground in readiness for the inevitable wind.

Beyond the village, the peninsula of Sagres hangs above a potentially angry ocean. Since prehistoric times the mood of the place, called the **Sacred Promontory,** has stirred the imagination. It was believed to be the sleeping place of the gods. If a man wanted to brood, he'd have plenty of room to pace on this plateau, far from distractions; which may help to explain why Henry the Navigator would have chosen this site for his 15th-century "think tank", the so-called School of Navigation.

Tantalizing scraps of evidence cast the prince's shadow over the promontory: fortress **walls** and buildings, an old **chapel,** and stones laid out in the form of a large mariners' **compass** or sundial. The Portuguese say that all the buildings were sacked in 1587 by a squadron commanded by Sir Francis Drake. (The English, among others, were then at war with Spain; Portugal at the time was under Spanish administration.)

On Sacred Promontory of Sagres, Prince Henry's "students" may have pondered principles of navigation with stone compass and sundial.

Some of the fortress walls, believed to date from the era of Prince Henry, have been restored. You can drive inside the fortifications via a curving tunnel just big enough for the excursion coaches to inch through (to the admiring applause of the passengers on occasion). You can walk to the edge of the cliff and look at the waves more than 200 feet straight down. Or you can join the local anglers dropping a very long line over the side. (This place also seems to be a favourite of lobsters.) The ruins of the compound's principal buildings have been rebuilt and transformed into a youth hostel. Jeans hang out to dry on the windward side of

Saintly Odyssey

Cape St. Vincent is named after a 4th-century Christian martyr, a Spanish priest killed at the time of the Diocletian persecution by the Roman governor of Valencia.

When the Moslems invaded Iberia the body was transferred to the Algarve's "sacred promontory". But it, too, was overrun by the Moors.

The saint's relics were recovered in the 12th century. Legend says a couple of ravens hovered over the hiding place, pointing it out to the searchers sent by Portugal's first king. As the relics were carried back to Lisbon, the devoted ravens flew along with the ship.

The seal of the city of Lisbon shows a sailing ship with a black bird fore and aft.

what might have been Prince Henry's headquarters.

And finally to **Cape St. Vincent,** "the end of the world". This intensely bleak cliff was the last sight of Europe for those explorers setting forth on fearsome voyages beyond the horizon. Today ships are almost always in view—leisurely freighters and fast-moving super-tankers and warships. About 200 ships a day turn this corner on the main highway between the Mediterranean and the north Atlantic.

The best place to watch all the traffic is the outdoor observation platform circling the famous **lighthouse** of Cape St. Vincent (if you're up to the 73 steps of the inevitably spiral staircase inside the tower). The buildings here belonged to a Franciscan convent, which was abandoned in 1834. In 1846, construction of the lighthouse began. Originally there was a battery of paraffin lamps; electricity arrived in 1906. In the daytime you can climb up for a close look at the 3,000-watt bulbs and the prisms which concentrate their beams. The light is visible 60 miles away. So many tourists come to inspect the lighthouse that a small souvenir stand operates in the base of the tower.

Seven lighthouse-keepers and their families live in the remodeled quarters of the compound. With Portuguese understatement they say it's a nice place to live because the air is pure. But looking down from the cliff, even on the calmest day, you can sense the cataclysmic force stored in the Atlantic. This is one of the very few points of the Algarve coast where you won't be tempted to take a dip.

Excursion to Lisbon

Until the 19th century, the overland voyage from the Algarve to Lisbon took a week or more. Now it's only half a day by train or express bus and 40 minutes by air. Various firms run excursions from the Algarve resorts to Lisbon, usually package tours by coach which include sightseeing, meals and one night at a hotel in the capital.

Like the Portuguese people, Lisbon is an unpretentious city with quiet charm. As European capitals go, it's an easy-going city with manageable traffic jams and air that's actually breathable. Lisbon has a generous share of first-class monuments. But churches, museums and other serious pursuits are by no means the whole story. There's nothing high-brow about its fascinating port, medieval residential district or down-to-earth nightlife. Beyond Lisbon the guided tours normally include sidetrips to the nearby Estoril coast and the lovable hill town of Sintra.

Climbing hills by standing still: Victorian Santa Just lift makes easy work of it in central Lisbon.

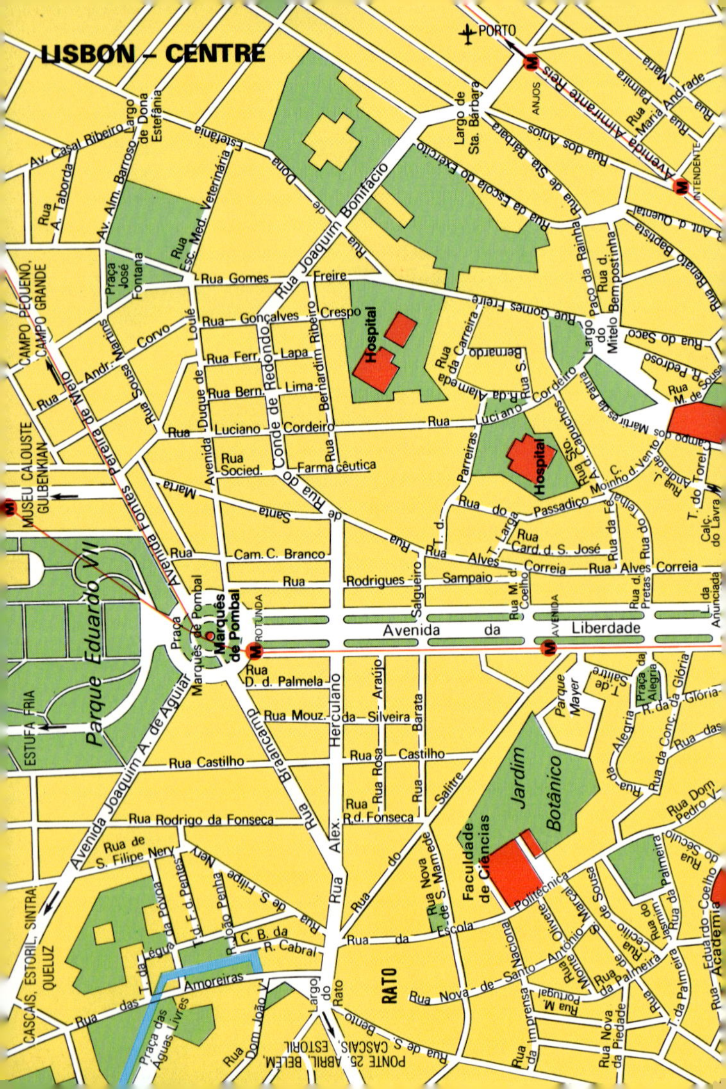
LISBON – CENTRE
PORTO
ANJOS
INTENDENTE
Avenida Almirante Reis
Rua Maria Andrade
Rua Palmira
Rua Maria
Rua dos Anjos
Largo de Sta. Bárbara
Rua de Sta. Bárbara
Rua da Escola do Exército
Rua Ant. d. Quental
Rua Renato Baptista
Av. Casal Ribeiro
Largo de Dona Estefânia
Rua Dona Estefânia
Av. Alm. Barroso
Rua A. Taborda
Rua Esc. Med. Veterinária
Praça José Fontana
Rua Joaquim Bonifácio
Rua de Dona
Rua Gomes Freire
Rua Gonçalves Crespo
Rua Ferr. Lapa
Rua Bern. Lima
Rua Conde de Redondo
Rua Bernardim Ribeiro
Hospital
Rua da Carreira
Alameda
R. da
Rua S. Bernardo
Rua Luciano Cordeiro
Largo Paço da Rainha
Rua d. Bempostinha
Largo do Mitelo
Rua do Saco
R. Pedroso
Rua M. de Sousa
Rua Mártires da Pátria
Campo dos Mártires
CAMPO PEQUENO, CAMPO GRANDE
Rua Andr.
Rua Sousa Martins
Rua Corvo
Loulé
Rua Pereira de Melo
Avenida Duque de Loulé
Rua Socied. Farmacêutica
Rua Luciano Cordeiro
Rua Sto. Capuchos
Rua d. Passadiço
Moinho d. Vento
Rua J. Andrade
T. do Torel
Calç. do Lavra
Parreiras
MUSEU CALOUSTE GULBENKIAN
Avenida Fontes
Rua Marta
Rua Santa
Rua de Rua do
Rua Cam. C. Branco
Rua Rodrigues Sampaio
Rua Alves Correia
Rua Alves Correia
T. d.
T. Larga
Rua Card. d. S. José
Rua da Fé
Rua do Telhal
Rua M. d. Coelho
Rua d. Pretas
L. da Anunciada
Salgueiro
Parque Eduardo VII
Praça Marquês de Pombal
Marquês de Pombal
ROTUNDA
Avenida da Liberdade
AVENIDA
Rua D. d. Palmela
Rua Mouz. da Silveira
Araújo
Herculano
Barata
Braancamp
Parque Mayer
T. de Salitre
Praça da Alegria
R. da Glória
Rua da Glória
Rua das
Rua da Alegria
Rua da Conc. da Glória
ESTUFA FRIA
Avenida Joaquim A. de Aguiar
Rua Castilho
Rua Rosa Castilho
Salitre
Jardim Botânico
Rua Rodrigo da Fonseca
Rua R.d. Fonseca
Rua Alex.
Rua de S. Filipe Nery
Rua Nova de S. Mamede
Faculdade de Ciências
Politécnica
Rua Dom Pedro V
Rua do Século
Rua da Palmeira
Rua do Jasmim
Rua Eduardo Coelho
Academia
T. d. F. d. Pentes
Légua da Póvoa
João Penha
C. B. da
R. Cabral
Rua da Escola
Rua Marçal
Rua Oliveira
Rua de Sousa
Rua Cecílio de Sousa
Rua Monte Olivete
Rua Nova de Santo António
Rua da Imprensa Nacional
Rua M. Portugal
Rua Nova da Piedade
CASCAIS, ESTORIL, SINTRA, QUELUZ
Rua das Amoreiras
T. da
Praça das Águas Livres
Rua Dom João V
Largo do Rato
RATO
Rua de S. Bento
PONTE 25 ABRIL, BELEM, CASCAIS, ESTORIL

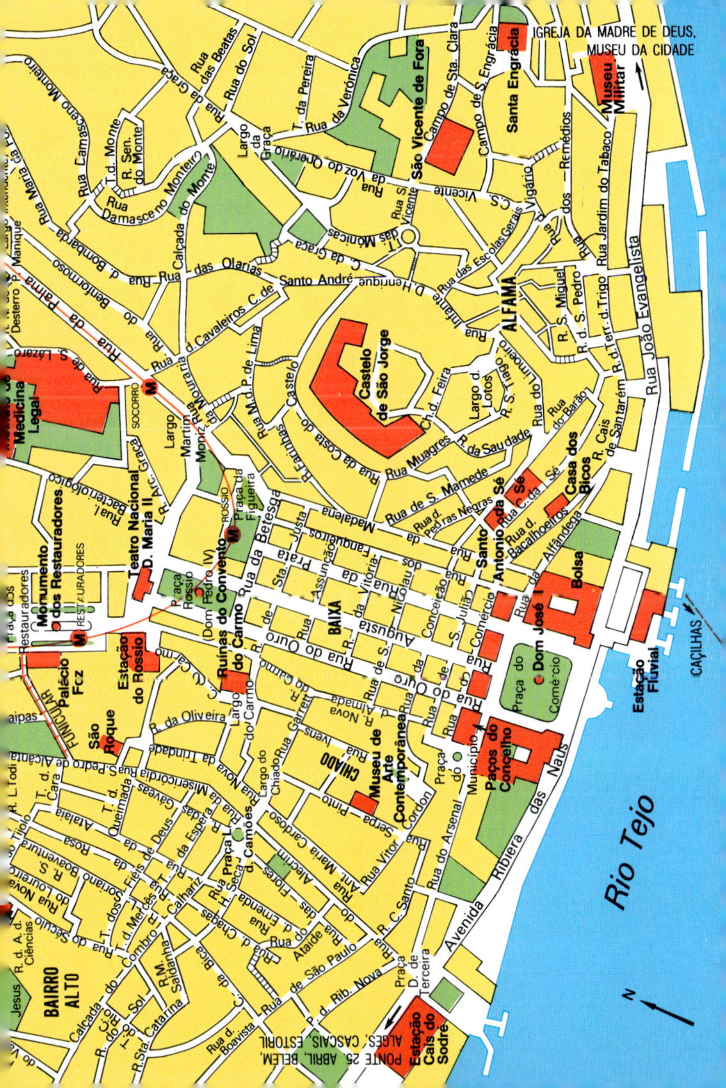

IGREJA DA MADRE DE DEUS, MUSEU DA CIDADE
Museu Militar
Santa Engrácia
Campo de S. Engrácia
Campo de Sta. Clara
São Vicente de Fora
Rua da Verónica
T. da Pereira
Rua do Sol
Rua das Beatas
Rua da Graça
Largo da Graça
Rua da Voz do Operário
Rua Damasceno Monteiro
Calçada do Monte
R. Sen. do Monte
T.d. Monte
Rua Maria da Fonte
Rua d. Bombarda
Rua do Benformoso
Rua das Olarias
C. da Graça
T. das Mónicas
Rua S. Vicente
C.S. Vicente
Vigário
Rua dos Remédios
Rua Jardim do Tabaco
Rua das Escolas Gerais
Rua D. Henrique
Rua Infante
Santo André
Rua d. Cavaleiros
C. de Santo André
Desterro
Rua da Palma
Rua de S. Lázaro
Instituto de Medicina Legal
SOCORRO
Largo Martim Moniz
Rua da Mouraria
Rua M.d. P. de Lima
Rua do Castelo
Castelo de São Jorge
Ch.d. Feira
Largo d. Lotos
R. S. Tiago
Rua do Limoeiro
Rua do Barão
ALFAMA
R. S. Miguel
R. d. S. Pedro
R. d. Terr. d. Trigo
Rua João Evangelista
R. Cais de Santarém
Rua da Costa do Castelo
Rua Muagres
R. da Saudade
Rua de S. Mamede
Rua d. Pedras Negras
Sé
Rua C. da Sé
Casa dos Bicos
Rua d. Bacalhoeiros
Rua da Alfândega
Santo António da Sé
Rua da Madalena
Rua dos Fanqueiros
Rua da Betesga
Praça da Figueira
ROSSIO
Teatro Nacional D. Maria II
Rua I. Bacteriologico
Monumento dos Restauradores
Praça dos Restauradores
RESTAURADORES
Praça Rossio (Dom Pedro IV)
Rua da Prata
Rua dos Sapateiros
Rua da Assunção
Rua da Vitória
Rua dos Correeiros
Rua Augusta
BAIXA
Rua de S. Nicolau
Rua da Conceição
Rua de S. Julião
Rua do Comércio
Rua do Ouro
Rua da Alfândega
Dom José I
Bolsa
Praça do Comércio
Estação Fluvial
CAÇILHAS
Estação do Rossio
Ruínas do Carmo
Largo do Carmo
Palácio Foz
FUNICULAR
São Roque
R. da Oliveira
Rua da Trindade
Rua Nova da Trindade
Rua Garrett
Rua Nova d. Almada
Rua Ivens
Rua Serpa Pinto
CHIADO
Museu de Arte Contemporânea
Rua Vitor Cordon
Largo do Chiado
Praça L. d. Camões
Praça do Município
Paços do Concelho
Rua do Arsenal
Avenida Ribiera das Naus
Rio Tejo
Rua Ant. Maria Cardoso
Rua das Flores
Rua do Alecrim
Rua da Emenda
Rua das Chagas
R.M. Saldanha
Rua do Loreto
Rua da Misericórdia
Rua das Gáveas
Rua da Atalaia
Rua da Rosa
T. da Queimada
Rua da Barroca
Rua S. Pedro de Alcântara
T. d. Cara
Rua da Espera
Rua dos Fiéis de Deus
Rua d. Mercês
Rua do Calhariz
Calçada do Combro
Rua do Século
Rua Nova do Loureiro
Rua Soriano
R.S. Boaventura
R. d. A. d. Ciências
BAIRRO ALTO
Jesus
Rua do Sol
R.Sta. Catarina
Rua d. Boavista
Bica
Rua d. Ataíde
Rua de São Paulo
Rua C. Santo
Rua Rib. Nova
Praça D. de Terceira
Estação Cais do Sodré
PONTE 25. ABRIL, BELEM, ALGES, CASCAIS, ESTORIL
N

Seeing Lisbon

The legendary seven hills of Lisbon—actually a couple of dozen—provide many vantage points over the tile roofs, inviting parks and gardens and the great sweep of the harbour. Lisbon is situated on the most regal part of the Tagus river, which begins in eastern Spain and runs into the Atlantic a few miles down the estuary.

The age of exploration begun on the Algarve reached its climax in Lisbon during the reign of King Manuel (1495–1521). He sent Vasco da Gama round the Cape of Good Hope to India. And the king celebrated the discoveries by building impressive monuments. Two of the best are within walking distance of the modern Monument to the Discoveries in the district called Belém, from which the explorers set forth. The waterfront is nearly 20 miles long, but in Belém (which means Bethlehem) the sights are close together.

The most famous monument is the graceful **Torre de Belém,** a marvellous little 16th-century fortress with finely carved details built alongside an almost tropical park. Leaving the Torre and heading east, you'll come to the **Museu de Arte Popular,** also on the waterfront. Inside are examples of folk art

Year-round flower market thrives in Rossio square. Church, upper left, was ruined in 1755 quake.

and exhibits on the customs of Portugal arranged according to region. Fabrics, furniture, embroidery, toys and dolls are all on display. Near the museum, Lisbon's biggest religious monument, the **Mosteiro dos Jerónimos,** is a formidable example of Manueline architecture. Most of the monastery's vast limestone façade is unadorned, so the areas devoted to intricate carvings stand out all the more in contrast. The inside is spacious and the atmosphere is calm. The two-storey cloister is full of original details.

A short walk east of the monastery brings you to the **Museu Nacional dos Coches** occupying the former royal riding school. Even small children usually maintain their interest in this museum full of ceremonial coaches and carriages in which kings and diplomats travelled during four centuries.

Another museum, between Belém and the central district of Lisbon, is the **Museu Nacional de Arte Antiga** (National Museum of Ancient Art). The 15th-century polyptych the *Ad-*

oration of St. Vincent by Nuno Gonçalves is the star attraction in the museum's collection. King Afonso V, Prince Henry the Navigator, Queen Isabel, Prince João, and many other contemporary portraits of Portuguese society: fishermen, beggars, bishops, knights as well as the saint himself, make these six panels a precious historic document as well as a work of art.

Hieronymus Bosch, Hans Holbein the Elder and Dürer are among many other artists whose works are on display.

Of all the museums in Lisbon, the most remarkable is the **Calouste Gulbenkian** collection. The oil billionaire, who died in Lisbon in 1955, acquired thousands of important works of art, from Egyptian sculpture to Impressionist paintings. The best of everything is displayed in a comfortable modern building set in its own lush park.

For respite from purely cultural endeavours, soak up the local colour in the extremely hilly **Alfama** section of Lisbon,

Museum Finder

We have mentioned several museums worth visiting on an excursion to Lisbon from the Algarve. For those with more time to spare, a quick reference guide to the city's top ten museums is provided below.

Most Lisbon museums are open Tuesdays to Sundays from about 10 a.m. to 5 p.m. Be sure to check local listings for any seasonal changes in opening hours.

Ancient Art—Museu Nacional de Arte Antiga, Rua das Janelas Verdes. Open later Thursdays and Sundays.

Archaeology—Museu Arqueológico (Carmo), Convento do Carmo. Largo do Carmo.

Coaches—Museu Nacional dos Coches, Praça Afonso de Albuquerque. Belém. Open later in summer.

Decorative Arts—Museu Escola de Artes Decorativas (Fundacão Ricardo Espirito Santo Silva). Largo das Portas do Sol 2, Alfama. Closes 1–2 p.m. weekdays; on Sundays, closed in the morning.

Folk Art—Museu de Arte Popular. Avenida Brasília. Belém.

Gulbenkian—Museu Calouste Gulbenkian. Avenida de Berna at Praça de Espanha. Hours change in summer.

Military—Museu Militar. Largo dos Caminhos de Ferro. Opens later on Sundays.

Naval—Museu da Marinha. Praça do Império.

Religious Art—Museu de Arte Sacra, next to São Roque, Largo Trindade Coelho.

Tiles—Museu do Azulejo. Convento da Madre de Deus. Closes 1–2.30 p.m.

For further details on all these museums, consult the Berlitz LISBON travel guide.

which hasn't changed much since the Moorish occupation. The old stone houses lean and tilt quite haphazardly, the streets zig and zag, and daily life passes before your eyes—quaint or boisterous, always fascinating. At night the husky voices of black-shawled singers are heard in the *fado* nightclubs, pouring forth music that sounds right at home in Lisbon's oldest neighbourhood.

Back at the riverside, the **Praça do Comércio** is an enormous square lined on three sides by arcaded buildings; the fourth side is open to the harbour. From here to the less extravagant but livelier main square of Lisbon, the **Rossio**, the streets are laid out in rectangular form. The plan for this district, called the Baixa (lowland), was devised by the Marquis of Pombal, who rebuilt Lisbon from the rubble of the 1755 earthquake.

From the Rossio district northward runs the Avenida da Liberdade, a boulevard with 12 traffic lanes, gardens, ponds, fountains, statues and mosaic pavements. Beyond a tall

Lisbon cityscapes mix old and new architecture plus statues galore.

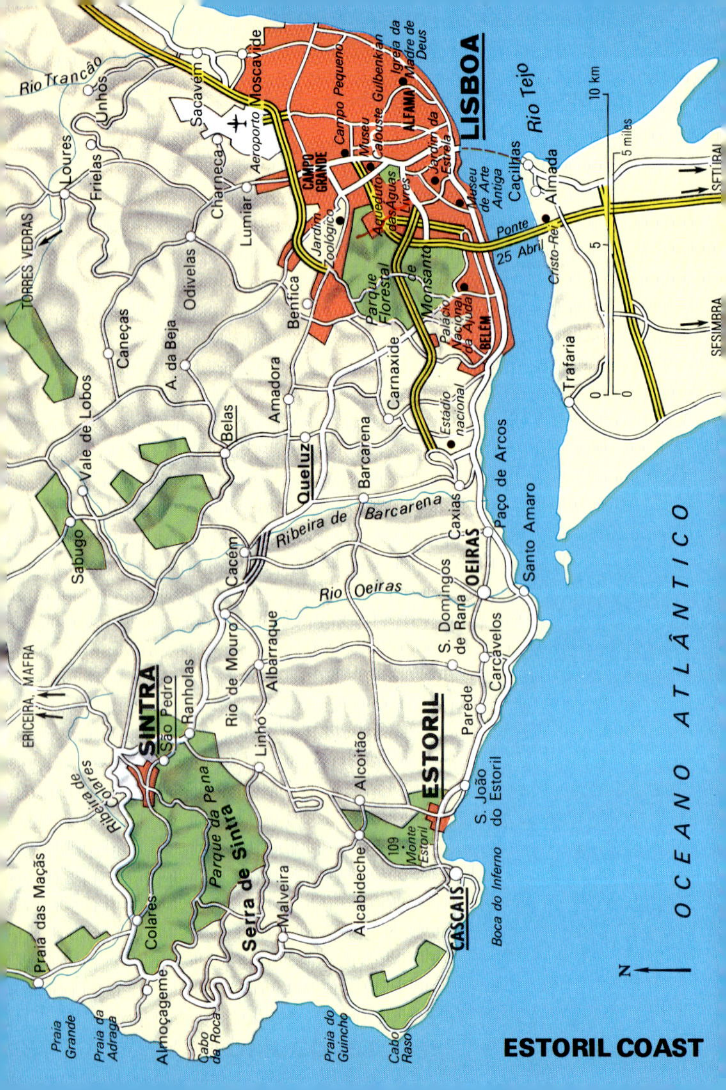

ESTORIL COAST

statue of Pombal himself, the formal Edward VII park continues uphill.

Standing high above the city, the **Castelo de São Jorge** (St. George's castle) was probably begun by the Romans. The ramparts now surround a delightful park stocked with peacocks, pheasants, pelicans and, especially, ravens—the symbols of Lisbon.

Estoril Coast

Excursions follow the coast west from Lisbon, as the riverfront evolves into a series of Atlantic Ocean beaches. The most famous is **Estoril,** a resort about 15 miles from Lisbon. This cosmopolitan area was a haven for Europe's ex-kings in the first half of this century. Victorian villas and modern mansions can be glimpsed behind barriers of shrubs, vines and trees. The new casino combines a nightclub, restaurants, bars, exhibition halls, cinema and a gambling operation big enough to keep 200 croupiers busy.

In contrast to Estoril's formality, **Cascais** is a happy combination of a working fishing port and a residence for aristocrats and just plain holidaymakers. Overlooking the main swimming/fishing beach, the 13th-century citadel is one of the few buildings to have survived the quake and tidal wave of 1755.

Sintra

Finally excursions turn inland to the fetching hill town of Sintra. Since the 14th century, Portuguese kings have made the **Paço da Vila** their summer home. This royal palace, right in the centre of town, is topped by two gigantic conical chimneys. When you tour the establishment you'll discover that they are attached to the kitchen; their ventilation was required when roasting all those oxen for a medieval banquet.

A more eccentric palace, the **Palácio da Pena,** overlooks the town from a hilltop so high that kings in residence could gloat over a view of their domain all the way from Lisbon to the Atlantic. The architecture mixes Gothic, Manueline, Renaissance and Moorish styles though most of the construction was done in the 19th century.

On a nearby hilltop, the **Castelo dos Mouros** (Moors' Castle) dates from the 8th or 9th century. Its capture by the forces of Afonso Henriques in 1147 was considered a triumphal breakthrough in the reconquest of Portugal from the Moslems.

What to Do

Sports

Thanks to the admirable climate and coastline, almost all sports enthusiasts find what they're looking for in the Algarve—whether it be a challenging round of golf or a lazy paddle in sea or pool. With about 100 miles of southward-facing beaches to exploit, the accent is obviously on water sports. But the region is geared to satisfy the demands of sports-lovers ashore as well.

Water Sports

All Portuguese beaches are free and open to the public without restriction. Of course you'll be charged if you want to use beach-chairs, umbrellas, awnings or other comforts, which are often available.

Life-guards are stationed at some, but by no means all, beaches. A green flag flying means the sea is calm and a life-guard is on duty. A green flag above a chequered flag means the conditions are safe but there is no supervision. A yellow flag urges caution, and a red flag warns bathers to stay ashore.

The big beaches are sometimes divided into several zones to avoid conflicts of interest: one area for ball-playing, another for umbrellas and beach chairs.

The profusion of isolated coves may suggest the possibility of nude bathing. However, tourist offices post a multilingual notice recalling that nudity is outlawed on Portuguese

beaches. Recently enforcement has not been notably aggressive, but it can be.

The exhilaration of pollution-free transport: young student riders ramble through Vilamoura's woods.

Snorkelling. Masks, breathing tubes, fins and spear-guns are sold at resorts along the coast, usually at reasonable prices. The rock formations off the westerly Barlavento coast provide fascinating undersea sightseeing and attract fish in abundance.

Scuba diving. Considering the splendours of the sea-cliffs and ocean grottoes, the sport has not reached its full poten-

Daniel Vittet, Genève

tial here. But equipment and instruction are available in Alvor, Luz Bay and Lagos. Compressors are found in many towns.

Sailing and boating. Sailing dinghies may be hired at a number of resorts and beaches; some places also offer instruction. At the Vilamoura marina, sailing boats large and small may be rented, as well as motorboats with and without driver. Yachtsmen can find anchorage, fuel and water in half a dozen Algarve ports but the region's only all-weather safe harbour with full facilities for pleasure boats is Vilamoura. Yachts up to 150 feet long are moored as a matter of course but even bigger vessels can be accommodated.

Water-skiing. Some of the major resorts have boats, skis and instructors. If ocean conditions are unpromising, there are protected estuaries and lagoons here and there between Portimão and Vila Real.

Windsurfing. This exciting sport for well-balanced sailors has caught on all along the Algarve coast; experienced windsurfers can rent a rig and newcomers can sign up for tuition. Five to seven hours, they claim, can transform a soaking-wet tyro into a stand-up whiz.

Fishing. Plenty of sizable Atlantic fish are just waiting for Algarve anglers off beaches and cliffs. In several resorts you can rent a small boat with rod and reel in the bargain. For shark, marlin and tuna (or if you don't catch any, at least the fun of the day), sign up for one of the deep-sea excursions. They leave day and night from Vilamoura, Portimão and Sagres. There are also light-hearted fishing trips where the emphasis is as much on the food and drink as the sport, and all manner of lazy sight-seeing trips up and down the coast by motor-launches and sailing ships.

Sports Ashore

Golf. The publicity brochures call the Algarve "Golfer's Paradise" because of the climate and the profusion of clubs. A glance at the six championship courses, reading from west to east:

Palmares (near Lagos): 18 holes. Challenging holes on the dunes and long cliffs with ocean panorama.

Penina (near Portimão): 18 holes. Longest and oldest Algarve course with a distinguished history of championships. Woods and water hazards. There are also two 9-hole courses.

Vilamoura (near Quarteira):

18 holes. Millions of gallons of Vilamoura water keep it evergreen. Most fairways chop through umbrella pines.

Dom Pedro, Vilamoura: 18 holes. The younger of the courses in this huge development; plenty of sea views.

Vale do Lobo (near Quarteira): 27 holes. Rugged terrain provides much interest, especially the spectacular 7th hole, par 3, a real cliffhanger.

Quinta do Lago (near Faro). 27 holes. American-designed with roomy fairways and lush greens kept verdant by computer-controlled sprinkling.

Minigolf. If it's too hot for the real thing, half a dozen hotels and resorts have little links for diversion.

Tennis. At last count more than 70 all-weather courts were in operation at Algarve hotels and "tourist villages". At many places equipment can be hired and instruction is available.

Riding. The terrain of beaches and woods and easy hills makes the Algarve a happy little world for horses and their riders. Stables (and instructors) are found all along the coast.

And if you're just watching, there are spectator sports for all tastes: golf and tennis tournaments, horse shows, yacht regattas and speedboat racing.

Festivals and Folklore

Don't expect festivals in the same class as the Carnival in Rio—Portugal is much too sober. But every town does have a festival at least once a year, on its saint's day, and you wouldn't want to miss the charm. Check at the tourist office when you arrive for the calendar of coming events.

At any *festa* there is likely to be a solemn religious procession only slightly jarred by the fireworks, American-style majorettes and volunteer firemen holding polished ceremonial axes. It all leads to plenty of country-fair entertainment—games of chance, children's rides, candy floss, *cachorros quentes* (hot dogs), and dancing in the streets. The most elaborate and free-wheeling Algarve festival is the Carnival in Loulé. But every town's fair, no matter how modest, is fun.

Folklore shows are regularly staged in the big hotels. This is an easy introduction to the costumes, music and dancing of the Algarve countryside.

The girls wear black felt hats over bright scarves, with colourful blouses and aprons over skirts with horizontal stripes. High-button shoes go over white knit stockings. In the swift whirling dances it's

Algarve folk dancer adjusts scarf before donning a man's black hat.

revealed they also wear long underwear in spite of the climate. The men are dressed more drably, with trousers, waistcoats, cummerbunds and flat hats all in black.

The singers are accompanied by accordions and triangles. There are two kinds of dances: the *corridinho* or jig, whirlwind fast with stamping feet, and the *bailes de roda*, reels or square dances. Don't be surprised if the hospitable Algarve dancers invite you to join the stomping, hand-clapping party.

Bullfights

In Portugal the star of the bullfighting team, inaccurately called a matador (slaughterer), taunts and finally dominates the bull, but the animal always leaves the ring alive. This makes Portuguese bullfights less conclusive than the classic Spanish version.

The matador, dressed like a peacock and just as haughty, takes on the half-ton beast armed only with a red cape and a symbolic sword. Lacking the intervention of picadors and the "moment of truth", this may seem just a watered-down version of a Spanish bullfight. But it contains flashes of colour and music and even drama.

Some of the bulls are fought in the old Portuguese style *(à antiga portuguesa)*, which has elements of a circus, a horse-show and a rodeo. Bullfighters in 18th-century costumes, mounted on fearless, high-stepping horses arouse the bulls, outrun and outwit them. During each chase the *cavaleiro* (horseman) leans down and stabs the bull's shoulder with a long dart. When the quota of darts has been planted, the horseman raises his three-cornered hat to the crowd and leaves the field in triumph. Some of the *cavaleiros* are as glamorous as film idols, but others unashamedly show their bald pates at the final salute.

The second act of each fight *à antiga* turns to roughhouse. Eight young volunteers called *forcados* leap into the ring, alone together with the angry, dart-infested bull. Though the bull's horns have been padded he can still do dreadful damage. The *forcados* have to prompt the bull to attack them at exactly the right moment so

that their strategy works and they can subdue the animal with their bare hands. It doesn't always succeed on the first try!

Bullfights traditionally begin on the dot at 5 p.m. but in the peak tourist season, the Algarve bull rings make an exception because of the heat. The midsummer *corridas* at Vila Real de Santo António, Albufeira and Portimão are run under the lights starting at 10 p.m.

Nightlife

The after-dark scene along the Algarve coast can lure you to a fishermen's bar or the elegance of a casino or floating nightclub. Between those extremes you are almost certain to find just the kind of mood you're looking for: indoors or outdoors, romantically obscure or cheerfully bright, moodily quiet or robustly amplified, bar or *boîte*, pub or club, lounge or disco.

Three **casinos** operate in the Algarve: at Alvor, Vilamoura and Monte Gordo. They have restaurants with nightly high-stepping floor-shows, and the gambling facilities are open from 3 or 5 p.m. until 3 a.m. (Be sure to take your passport; gentlemen are requested to wear jackets in the evening.) The games available are roulette, blackjack, baccarat and the Portuguese game called "French bank". Slot machines stand by to recycle any excess profits.

Semi-professional **folklore** ensembles often perform the rousing dances of the Algarve on special nights at the hotels. Another popular attraction is the "*fado* night" at which this most distinctively Portuguese music is sung and played. Some visitors (and Portuguese, too) are immune to the *fado*'s melancholy charms, but with luck you'll fall under the spell of the throbbing voice of a woman all in black, singing of lost love or longing for the past, or the future.

The Algarve **cinema** scene focuses on rather out-of-date films of many nationalities. But tickets are cheap. The films are almost always shown with the dialogue in the original language and sub-titles in Portuguese.

Tourists join costumed experts in noisy, hand-clapping Algarve dances. Cheerfully decorated ceramics, above, are among favourite souvenirs.

Shopping

The shops of the Algarve are well stocked with trinkets and souvenirs as well as works of art and useful items for your home, yourself or as special gifts. If you don't find what you're looking for in the chic boutiques, go to the country markets. Or try and find the artisans where they work.

What to buy

Azulejos. These hand-painted glazed tiles decorate palaces and humble cottages, churches and bars all over Portugal. You can buy a single square with a pretty Algarvian motif or a whole set for your patio or kitchen.

Brass, bronze and **copper.** Candlesticks, old-fashioned scales, pots and pans, bowls and trays. (You may even find a small still suitable for making bathtub gin.)

Cork. Portugal is the world's leading producer. Placemats, intricate sculptures and lightweight knick-knacks.

Dolls. In the authentic costumes of the Algarve and other regions of Portugal.

Embroidery. The delicate needlework of the island of Madeira is admired everywhere and sold in the Algarve. Local products in a similar if less subtle vein are also on sale.

Filigree. Fine threads of sil-

ver or gold are worked into brooches, pendants, pins and earrings in Portuguese designs such as caravelles, bullfighters or roosters, or the universal shapes of butterflies, hearts and flowers.

Ironwork. Though heavy going on the baggage scales, wrought-iron lamps, flower-pot holders and weather-cocks are worth considering.

Knitwear. Hand-knit pullovers or rugged fishermen's sweaters—or a woollen shawl fit for a *fado* singer.

Leather. Quality and prices are interesting in shoes, wallets, belts and bags.

Marble. The unusual texture of the local stone makes for attractive vases, candlesticks and ashtrays.

Pottery. From the simplest earthenware pots for kitchen or garden to the most artistic hand-painted plates and bowls, the Algarve is a happy hunting ground for all ceramics.

Roosters. Brightly hand-painted statuettes of ceramic or wood, honouring Portugal's favourite bird. The legend says a cock arose from a judge's dinner plate and crowed to proclaim the innocence of an unjustly accused man.

Rugs. Mostly from the Alentejo,* hand-made as they've been for centuries, in cheerful colours and designs.

Seashells. Huge shells and coral for collectors; not from local waters but imported from former Portuguese territories in the tropics. Also locally made seashell "sculptures"—statuettes of fishermen or sailing boats ingeniously composed of tiny shells.

Sweets. Marzipan and figs are the basis for typical Algarve sweets, often produced in the whimsical form of fruits or animals.

Wicker. Bags, mats, hats, trays, plant-holders, glass-holders, furniture...

Wines. Don't forget to take home a bottle of one of the legendary Portuguese wines—port from the Douro Valley or Madeira from the Atlantic island. They come in aperitif and after-dinner versions. Or choose one of the local liqueurs, of honey or the arbutus berry.

Woodwork. Furniture...or even a genuine shepherd's crook.

Earthenware pots at weekly market in Loulé make for lengthy deliberations. You can't take them all!

---

* The region between the Algarve and Lisbon.

Wining and Dining

Most Algarve cooking is as unaffected as a fishermen's barbecue: grilled or fried fish, straightforward chops or charcoal-broiled chicken. But serious gourmets needn't despair. There are some surprising exceptions to the modest style, most notably *cataplana*—as deliciously inventive as sweet-and-sour-pork.

The seafood, as fresh as the morning tide, is no longer amazingly cheap. In general, though, appetites and budgets are very well served in the restaurants of the Algarve. And the good, inexpensive local wine rounds out the happy, wholesome picture.

Choosing a Restaurant

Government inspectors rate all Portuguese restaurants according to a scale of four categories from luxury *(de luxo)* down to third class *(terceira classe)*. The rating isn't necessarily related to the quality of the food, but the higher the official class, the more the restaurant is permitted to charge. A sign announcing the class is usually affixed outside the restaurant, a menu in the window or beside the door lets you know what to expect in variety and price. Though the prices normally include all taxes and a service charge, you may want to leave an additional 5 to 10 per cent tip if the service was good.

If you choose to eat only in your hotel dining room, you may soon become bored with the colourless "international cuisine". Venturing forth into real Portuguese restaurants, you will almost certainly pay less for food that's more interesting and quite possibly tastier.

Meal Times

Breakfast *(o pequeno almoço)* is eaten anytime until about 10 a.m. Lunch *(o almoço)* is served from midday till about 3 p.m. Dinner *(o jantar)* tends to be eaten much earlier than across the border, in Spain—from about 7.30 to 9.30 p.m. If you find yourself feeling hungry later than that, try a *cervejaria*, one of the draught-beer snack-bars which stay open late with seafood and sandwiches.

Breakfast

The Portuguese eat a light breakfast: coffee, toast or rolls, butter and jam. Hotels can provide all the extras—juice, eggs, bacon or whatever else is required to duplicate an English or American breakfast.

Starters

Lunch and dinner often get off to a hearty start:

Caldo verde (green soup), a thick broth of potato purée and finely shredded cabbage or kale, usually includes a slice of sausage.

Canja de galinha: chicken and rice soup.

Gaspacho: the Algarve version of the famous cold soup of tomatoes, cucumbers and peppers.

Melão com presunto: the best part of this sophisticated combination is that both the melon and the smoked ham come from nearby farms.

Seafood

The prawns, crabs and fresh fish are their own best advertisement, so many seafood restaurants keep refrigerated display cases in the front window. You may also encounter trays of baby clams outside, very much alive and occasionally aiming jets of water into the air, or towards a customer, like infinitesimal whales. Shellfish are generally sold by weight not per portion; the menu lists the price in escudos per kilogram and you decide how hun-

Charcoal grill at seaside adds delicious flavour to Algarve lunch.

gry you are. Some promising ideas:

Amêijoas na cataplana: the Algarve's most dazzling culinary idea is named after the vessel in which it is cooked, a primitive predecessor of a pressure cooker. The ingredients are cockles (clams), sausage, ham, onion, garlic, paprika, chilli sauce, parsley and white wine. It would be a shame for anyone to leave the Algarve without trying this dish.

Açorda de marisco: a spicy, garlic-scented bread soup of seafood bits, baked in a casserole; raw eggs are folded into the mixture at the table.

Caldeirada de peixe: the Algarve version of bouillabaisse is a rich, filling fish stew you can eat with knife and fork.

Bacalhau: the Portuguese have been interested in cod ever since their first explorations to Newfoundland in 1501. Even though it comes dried, salted—and expensively—from distant seas, and even though some of the tastiest fresh fish in the world is right on the "doorstep", codfish is still the national dish. There seem to be hundreds of recipes. Look for *bacalhau à Gomes de Sá*, flaky chunks of cod baked with parsley, potatoes, onion and olives and garnished with grated hard-boiled egg.

Fresh seafood, home-made mural enhance pleasure of village meal.

Bife de atum: tunny (tuna) steak, a beefy fillet marinated in vinegar, salt, garlic and bay leaves, then cooked with onion and perhaps bacon.

Espadarte: swordfish also grills into a delicious steak. On some menus it's listed as *peixe agulha*. But don't confuse *espadarte* with *peixe espada*, a very long, thin fish sometimes translated "scabbard fish".

Sardinhas grelhadas: the aroma of sardines grilling over charcoal, which pervades the Algarve at times, may not rouse your appetite, but the end-product is delicious.

Otherwise, most fresh fish, whole or filleted, are served grilled. But the Portuguese are also fond of boiled fish dishes served with cabbage or green beans and boiled potatoes; they douse it all with oil and vinegar. Incidentally, salt and pepper are seldom set on the table in Portuguese restaurants. If you miss them, just ask the waiter for *"sal e pimenta, por favor"*.

Meat and Fowl

Bife na frigideira: is not what you think it means. A *frigideira* is a frying-pan, and this dish is

a beefsteak nicely done in a wine sauce.

Cabrito estufado: a casserole of kid, stewed with onions, potatoes, tomatoes and peas.

Carne de porco com amêijoas: a marvel of improbably compatible tastes—baby clams and chunks of pork—claimed as an Algarvian invention, even if most authorities give credit to the Alentejo region.

Coelho assado: roast rabbit with onions, white wine and seasoning.

Espetada mista: a Portuguese shish-kebab—chunks of beef, lamb and pork on a spit.

Feijoada: a far cry from the more elaborate national dish of Brazil, but still a filling stew of pigs' feet and sausage, white beans and cabbage.

Frango de churrasco: barbecued chicken, sometimes laced with spicy *piri-piri* sauce; the charcoal tang enhances the flavour of the meaty local birds.

Many dishes are served with *both* rice and potatoes as well as a token slice of tomato with a lettuce leaf.

Dessert

Doces regionais (regional sweets) interest travelling Portuguese the way local cheeses absorb the French. In the Algarve, almost every town has its own special cake or candy,

usually with a fanciful name and appearance. They come in the shape of birds, animals, fruits and vegetables. Among the most prominent ingredients are almonds, figs and eggs—all good fun for sweet-toothed holidays.

Other Portuguese desserts:

Arroz doce: rice pudding with cinnamon topping.

Pudim flan: caramel custard.

Pudim Molotov: the derivation of the name is obscure, but if you are tired of your slimming diet, you couldn't pick a more dramatic gesture than this calorific bomb of egg-white mousse in caramel sauce.

Or you may prefer Portuguese cheese *(queijo).* The richest is *Serra da Estrela,* cured ewe's-milk cheese from the country's highest mountain range. It takes a shepherdess some three hours to make each small cheese by hand. It is only available from December to April (though a harder, factory-made product *(Tipo Serra)* can be had year-round). Other cheeses on the menus are *Flamengo,* which resembles Edam, and *Saloio* and *Queijo Fresco,* creamy, cottage-cheese types, often served before the meal.

An excellent alternative ending for your meal is the fruit of the season. Restaurants serve

the best local products at their peak. Farm-fresh peaches, melons, strawberries and figs are a far cry from the bland supermarket fruits available in northern Europe.

Foreign Alternatives
Expatriates from several gastronomically interesting countries have opened restaurants in the Algarve. Secret native ingredients are not always available so authenticity may falter, but the cooks do try. Among the nationalities represented: Angolan, Chinese, Czechoslovakian, Dutch, French, Greek, Iranian, Italian, Vietnamese.

Table Wines
Portugal is one of those fortunate countries where all you really need to tell the waiter is *tinto* (red) or *branco* (white) and you can't go wrong. The *vinho da casa* (house wine) in any restaurant is bound to be drinkable, and maybe even first-rate. And if the choice of red or white isn't broad enough, you can order pink or green.

Vinho verde ("green wine") is named for its youth, not its colour. It's really a slightly sparkling, sharp white wine that goes especially well with seafood. A lesser-known variant from the same region in north-west Portugal bears the somewhat paradoxical name *vinho verde tinto* ("red green wine"). Both types should be served chilled.

So should rosé, which is better known abroad than at home; 80 per cent of all the bottles of Portuguese wine exported are rosé.

Vinho espumante, usually sweetish and frothy, is the Portuguese sparkling wine packaged suggestively in a Champagne-shaped bottle.

Of the local wines from the Algarve, you are most likely to be served *Lagoa*, which is produced in red, white and rosé. Beware of the unaccustomed alcoholic strength—about 13.5 degrees—which can certainly slow down anyone's afternoon in the hot sun. The wine from the other principal Algarve region, *Tavira*, is "only" 12.5 degrees, but still quite hearty.

A small linguistic problem: if you want a carafe of house wine rather than a bottle, don't ask for a *garrafa*. In Portuguese *garrafa* means bottle. A carafe is *um frasco*. But in any case bottled wine is inexpensive.

Other Drinks
The two most celebrated Portuguese drinks, port and Madeira, are produced in before- and after-dinner varieties.

From the Lagoa winery come two aperitif wines reminiscent of sherries—*Algar Seco* and *Afonso III*. They should be served chilled.

Portuguese beers are good. Light or dark, they are usually served chilled whether bottled or from the tap. A small draught beer is called *uma imperial;* a mug of draught beer is *uma caneca.*

Many brands of Portuguese mineral waters, bubbly or still, are available. Fruit juices are delicious. Most of the well-known soft drinks are on sale.

Several strong after-dinner drinks originate in the Algarve. The breathtaking *medronho* is distilled from the fruit of the arbutus tree. *Bagaço* or *bagaceira* (made out of grape residues) is also very powerful and similar to French *marc* or Italian *grappa*. *Brandymel,* a honey-based liqueur, tastes as if a swarm of bees went berserk in a distillery.

Coffee and Tea

At the end of lunch or dinner, most Portuguese order a *bica*, a small cup of black espresso coffee, either in the restaurant or a nearby café. With a few drops of milk in it, a *bica* is called a *garoto*. Cafés also serve white coffee in a tall glass, called a *galão*.

Tea *(chá)* has been drunk in Portugal ever since the local explorers introduced it to the western world.

To Help You Order...

Could we have a table? — **Queríamos uma mesa.**

I'd like a/an/some... — **Queria...**

beer	**uma cerveja**	mineral water	**água mineral**
bill	**a conta**	napkin	**um guardanapo**
bread	**pão**	pepper	**pimenta**
butter	**manteiga**	potatoes	**batatas**
coffee	**um café**	rice	**arroz**
dessert	**uma sobremesa**	salad	**uma salada**
fish	**peixe**	salt	**sal**
fruit	**fruta**	sandwich	**uma sanduíche**
ice-cream	**um gelado**	soup	**uma sopa**
meat	**carne**	sugar	**açúcar**
menu	**a ementa**	tea	**chá**
milk	**leite**	wine	**vinho**

alho	garlic	**gambas**	prawns (shrimp)
alperces	apricots	**gelado**	ice-cream
amêijoas	baby clams	**grão-de-bico**	chick-pea
ananás	pineapple	**guisado**	stew
arroz	rice	**lagosta**	spiny lobster
assado	roast	**laranja**	orange
atum	tunny (tuna)	**legumes**	vegetables
azeitonas	olives	**leitão**	suckling pig
bacalhau	codfish	**linguado**	sole
banana	banana	**lombo**	fillet
besugo	sea-bream	**lulas**	squid
bife (vaca)	beefsteak	**maçã**	apple
bolo	cake	**mariscos**	shellfish
borrego	lamb	**melancia**	watermelon
cabrito	kid	**mexilhões**	mussels
camarões	shrimp	**molho**	sauce
caracóis	snails	**morangos**	strawberries
caranguejo	crab	**ostras**	oysters
cavala	mackerel	**ovo**	egg
cebola	onion	**pargo**	bream
chouriço	a spicy sausage	**peixe**	fish
churrasco	grilled meat	**perú**	turkey
coelho	rabbit	**pescada**	hake
cogumelos	mushrooms	**pescadinha**	whiting
costeletas	chops	**pêssego**	peach
couve	cabbage	**porco**	pork
cozido	boiled	**presunto**	ham
dobrada	tripe	**queijo**	cheese
enguias, eiros	eels	**robalo**	bass
ervilhas	peas	**salmonete**	red mullet
estufado	braised	**salsichão**	large sausage
feijões	beans	**sardinhas**	sardines
figos	figs	**sobremesa**	dessert
framboesas	raspberries	**torrada**	toast
frango	chicken	**uvas**	grapes
frito	fried	**vitela**	veal

How to Get There

Because of the complexity and variability of the many fares, you should ask the advice of an informed travel agent well before your departure.

BY AIR

Scheduled flights

Though the Algarve's international airport at Faro handles some scheduled flights, it is mostly used for charter traffic. However, Lisbon is the main gateway to Portugal, both for European and intercontinental flights, and it has frequent connections to Faro.

Charter flight and package tours

From the U.K. and Ireland: The Algarve is an extremely popular package tour destination. Self-catering holidays proliferate to an equal extent. There are a tremendous number of flights available, but be sure to check booking conditions and regulations with your agent. The Algarve is ideal for golf, horse-riding and big-game fishing enthusiasts.

From North America: Tours are available to Lisbon in combination with Iberian or European destinations. For tours to Portugal and the Algarve only, you must either make independent air, transfer and hotel (plus car rental) arrangements, or book a fly/drive arrangement to Lisbon.

BY CAR

The main access road to Lisbon and the Algarve from France through Spain is at the western end of the Pyrenees. A motorway (expressway) runs from Biarritz (France) to Burgos. From there, take either the N1 to Madrid and continue on E4 via Badajoz and Setúbal to Lisbon, or the N620 and then the E3 via Valladolid, Salamanca, Guarda and Coimbra. There is a long-distance car-ferry service from Plymouth to Santander in northern Spain (a 24-hour trip). From Santander follow the N611 and then the E3 via Valladolid and Coimbra.

BY RAIL

There are two main routes to the Algarve via Paris and Lisbon (a journey of about 30–32 hours): via Hendaye (south-west France) and Fuentes de Onora/Vilar Formoso (Spanish/Portuguese frontier points) or via Aranda de Duero, Madrid and Valencia de Alcántara (frontier point). From the U.K., both routes offer a choice of sea crossings.

The *Inter-Rail Card* permits 30 days of unlimited rail travel in participating European countries to people under 26. The *Rail Europ Senior Card* is available for senior citizens and entitles the holder to a discount on European and internal Portuguese rail journeys. Anyone living outside Europe and North Africa can purchase a *Eurail-pass* for unlimited rail travel in 16 countries including Portugal (sign up before you leave home).

When to Go

The prettiest time of the year in the Algarve is during the springtime, January to April. The climate is generally warm in all seasons with extremes being rare. Winter evenings can sometimes be very chilly though, and hot periods in summer may feel stifling to persons who prefer milder weather. The table of average temperatures below will give you an idea of the climatic conditions most prevalent during the different months of the year.

		J	F	M	A	M	J	J	A	S	O	N	D
Air temperature	°C	12	12	14	15	18	21	23	24	22	18	15	13
	°F	54	54	57	59	64	69	73	75	72	64	59	55
Sea temperature	°C	15	16	17	18	19	21	21	20	19	18	16	14
	°F	59	61	62	64	66	69	69	67	66	64	61	57

Planning Your Budget

To give you an idea of what to expect, here are some average prices in Portuguese escudos. Remember that all prices must be regarded as approximate as inflation is running high.

Baby-sitters. 500 esc. per hour.

Bicycle hire. 500–1,000 esc. per day, 2,000 esc. per week.

Camping. 170 esc. per person with tent, 210 esc. per caravan (trailer).

Car hire (international company). *Morris Mini 1000* (2 doors) 1,800 esc. per day, 18 esc. per km., 19,600 esc. per week with unlimited mileage. *Renault 5 TL* (3 doors) 2,100 esc. per day, 21 esc. per km., 23,100 esc. per week with unlimited mileage. *Ford Escort Laser 1,3 L* (5 doors) 3,300 esc. per day, 33 esc. per km., 39,200 esc. per week with unlimited mileage. Add 16% tax.

Cigarettes. Portuguese brands from 120 esc., imported brands from 250 esc.

Entertainment. Bullfight 750–1,500 esc., cinema 250 esc., disco 500–2,000 esc., *fado* from 1,000 esc.

Golf. 3,000–4,000 esc. per day, set of clubs 1,000–2,500 esc. per game.

Guided tours. Full-day Algarve sightseeing around 2,500 esc., two-day Lisbon excursion, including hotel, around 11,000 esc.

Hairdressers. *Woman's* haircut 1,000 esc., shampoo and set 750 esc., manicure 150–500 esc. (some establishments charge far less). *Man's* haircut 300–1,000 esc.

Hotels (double room with bath per night at beach hotels). ***** 15,500–17,500 esc., **** 12,000–15,000 esc., *** 9,500–12,500 esc., ** 1,850–2,000 esc., * 1,200–1,400 esc. *Boarding house* 900–2,000 esc.

Meals and drinks. Continental breakfast 150–300 esc., lunch or dinner in fairly good establishment 1,000–4,000 esc., coffee 50–100 esc., beer 50–150 esc., Portuguese brandy 70–150 esc., gin and tonic 200–300 esc., bottle of wine 400 esc. and up.

Tennis. On average either 500 esc. per person per hour or 2,400 esc. per court.

Water-skiing. 1,500 esc. for 15 minutes.

Windsurfing (board hire). 600–1,200 esc. per hour.

BLUEPRINT for a Perfect Trip

An A-Z Summary of Practical Information and Facts

Contents

A star (*) following an entry indicates that relevant prices are to be found on page 103.

Listed after some basic entries is the appropriate Portuguese translation, usually in the singular, plus a number of phrases that should help you when seeking assistance.

AIRPORT *(aeroporto)*. Faro International Airport, serving the Algarve, is 7 kilometres by road from Faro, the regional capital. It's a 10-minute taxi ride to Faro, about half an hour to Albufeira. There is a bus service between the airport and Faro. Some resort hotels and package tour organizations send their vans or coaches to meet specific clients or groups. Porters and trolleys are available. **A**

Arriving passengers have a choice of several car hire firms maintaining service desks in the airport. There is a branch post office for mail, telegrams and telephone calls. A bank office, open late into the evening, handles currency exchange business. A tourist information office in the same area can help with hotel reservations, transport and other problems.

In the adjacent departure section of the terminal, an air-conditioned restaurant and bar are open 24 hours a day. There is also a newsstand-and-souvenir shop, and departing passengers on international flights may take advantage of a duty-free shop.

Airport information, tel. 23081.

Air Portugal information, tel. 25908.

Where can I get a taxi?	**Onde posso encontrar um táxi?**
Please take these bags.	**Leve-me a bagagem, por favor.**

BABY-SITTERS*. Most hotels and tourist villages organize baby-sitting at short notice. In the high season, especially for weekends, it's prudent to make arrangements well in advance. You may be charged extra for the hours after midnight and for the sitter's transport home. (Baby-sitters are not listed in the telephone directory in the Algarve; local facilities, when available, concern themselves primarily with the needs of working mothers in the daytime.) **B**

B

Portuguese children are taken almost everywhere, including restaurants, sometimes quite late at night.

Can you get me a baby-sitter for tonight?	**Pode encontrar-me uma baby-sitter para esta noite?**

BICYCLE HIRE* *(bicicletas de aluguer).* Reception desks at many hotels and tourist villages will be able to help you. Otherwise, ask at any local tourist information office for the address of a bicycle rental firm in the vicinity. In summer it's wise to limit strenuous riding to the cooler hours of the morning and late afternoon.

Motorbikes are also for hire in the Algarve.

I'd like to hire a bicycle.	**Queria alugar uma bicicleta.**
What's the charge per day?	**Qual é a tarifa por dia?**

C

CAMPING* *(campismo).* Most of the Algarve's camping sites are within easy distance of a beach. They range from extremely cheap, basic grounds to vast recreational centres with restaurants, pools and tennis courts.

You must register with your passport, as in a hotel, and at certain sites you are also required to show an official card identifying you as a member of a national or international camping association. Camping on beaches or anywhere outside recognized sites is illegal. Details on all Portuguese camping sites are contained in a brochure available at all tourist information offices, or consult:

Federação Portuguesa de Campismo, Rua Voz do Operário, 1, Lisbon 1000; tel. 862350.

Is there a camping site near here?	**Há algum parque de campismo por aqui perto?**
May we camp here?	**Podemos acampar aqui?**
We have a caravan (trailer).	**Temos uma roulotte.**

CAR HIRE* *(carros de aluguer).* Local car hire firms compete with the major international organizations at Faro Airport and principal resorts. Normally the prices are alike. You must be at least 23 years old to hire a car, and have a valid national (or an international) driving licence held for at least one year. If you present a recognized credit card, the deposit will be waived. Third-party insurance is included in the basic charge but a collision-damage waiver and personal accident policy may be added at extra cost. A government tax is assessed on the total amount of the rental.

I'd like to hire a car (tomorrow). — **Queria alugar um carro (para amanhã).**

for one day/a week — **por um dia/uma semana**

Please include full insurance. — **Que inclua um seguro contra todos os riscos, por favor.**

CIGARETTES, CIGARS, TOBACCO* *(cigarros, charutos, tabaco).* Cigarettes imported from Europe and the United States are sold for about three times as much as similar Portuguese brands. Among popular local makes are *SG, CT* and *Português Suave.* Cigarettes are sold at tobacco shops, news-stands, hotels, bars, etc. Tobacco shops also sell an ample range of Portuguese and imported cigars and pipe tobacco.

Smoking is prohibited in theatres and cinemas, indoor sports arenas and local buses. On inter-city buses, on journeys longer than one hour, smoking is permitted in the last three rows. Trains have smoking cars.

A packet of.../A box of matches, please. — **Um maço de.../Uma caixa de fósforos, por favor.**

filter-tipped — **com filtro**
without filter — **sem filtro**

CLOTHING. Pack a pullover, even in summer; the evenings can turn quite cool. But you won't need a raincoat. Winters are mild, though a topcoat might be welcome at night.

As for formality, if you plan to stay at a fancy hotel or patronize luxury restaurants, a certain degree of "dressing up" is to be expected. The casinos require men to wear jackets; ties are optional. But generally life is very informal along the coast.

If you're buying clothes in the Algarve—most tourists consider prices quite reasonable—note that shops in the resorts tend to charge more than in the towns.

Will I need a tie? — **É preciso gravata?**
Is it all right if I wear this? — **Vou bem assim?**

COMMUNICATIONS

Post offices are indicated by the letters CTT *(Correios, Telégrafos e Telefones).* Mail service generally is good but in the resort villages distribution can get bogged down under the seasonal load. If the post office is crowded or closed, you can buy stamps at many shops, such as tobacconists or souvenir stands. They usually display a sign, *Correios*. Most mailboxes on the street follow the British pillar-box design; they're painted bright red, too.

Post-office hours. Most local offices open from 9 a.m. to 12.30 p.m. and 2 to 6 p.m., Monday to Friday. Main offices are open from 8.30 a.m. to 6 or 6.30 p.m., Monday to Friday. The main post offices in Faro and Portimão are open on Saturday mornings as well.

Poste restante (general delivery). If you're not sure where you'll be staying in the Algarve, you can have mail sent *posta restante* to any post office convenient to you. For example:

Mr. John Smith, Posta Restante, 8200 Albufeira, Portugal

Be sure to take your passport or identity card when you go to pick up your letters from the *posta restante* window at the post office.

Telegrams *(telegrama)* can be sent from post offices, or you can give the text to your hotel receptionist. Many hotels have telex facilities and will transmit and receive messages for their guests, or you can use the public telexes in Faro and Portimão main post offices.

Telephone *(telefone)*. Automatic coin telephones are found in bars and restaurants and on the street in British-style square, closed-in phone boxes. Generally you must deposit several coins; unused ones are returned. You can dial most Western European countries direct or make international telephone calls through the clerk at any post office or at your hotel. Be prepared for lengthy delays in summer.

Dial 099 for the international operator and inquiries within Europe, 098 for the rest of the world.

Telephone Spelling Code

A	Aveiro	**J**	José	**S**	Setúbal
B	Braga	**K**	Kodak	**T**	Tavira
C	Coimbra	**L**	Lisboa	**U**	Unidade
D	Dafundo	**M**	Maria	**V**	Vidago
E	Évora	**N**	Nazaré	**W**	Waldemar
F	Faro	**O**	Ovar	**X**	Xavier
G	Guarda	**P**	Porto	**Y**	York
H	Horta	**Q**	Queluz	**Z**	Zulmira
I	Itália	**R**	Rossio		

Where's the nearest post office?	**Onde fica a estação de correios mais próxima?**
Have you received any mail for...?	**Tem correio para...?**
A stamp for this letter/ postcard, please.	**Um selo para esta carta/ este postal, por favor.**
express (special delivery)	**expresso**
airmail	**via aérea**
registered	**registado**
I want to send a telegram to...	**Quero mandar um telegrama para...**
Can you get me this number?	**Pode ligar-me para este número?**
reverse-charge (collect) call	**paga pelo destinatário**
person-to-person (personal) call	**com pré-aviso**

COMPLAINTS. If you've had no satisfaction from the manager of the shop, hotel or restaurant concerned, take your complaint to the nearest tourist office. They will either help sort them out or direct you to the nearest Consumer Information and Support Post, some 20 of which look after the consumers' rights and duties across the Algarve. If you have documents to support your claim, be sure to take them along.

CONSULATES and EMBASSIES *(consulado, embaixada).* A number of European countries have consuls or honorary consuls in the Algarve. For serious matters, people are usually referred to the embassy in Lisbon.

British consulates:	Rua Santa Isabel, 21, Portimão; tel. 23071.
	Rua General Humberto Delgado, 4, Vila Real de Santo António; tel. 43729.
Lisbon embassies	
Australia:	Avenida da Liberdade, 244; tel. 523350.
Canada:	Rua Rosa Araújo, 2; tel. 563821.
Eire:	Rua da Impresa a Estrella, 1; tel. 661569.
South Africa:	Avenida Luís Bivar, 10; tel. 535041.
United Kingdom:	Rua S. Domingos à Lapa, 37; tel. 661191.
U.S.A.:	Avenida Forças Armadas, 16; tel. 725600.

CONVERTER CHARTS. For fluid and distance measures, see page 111. Portugal uses the metric system.

C

Temperature

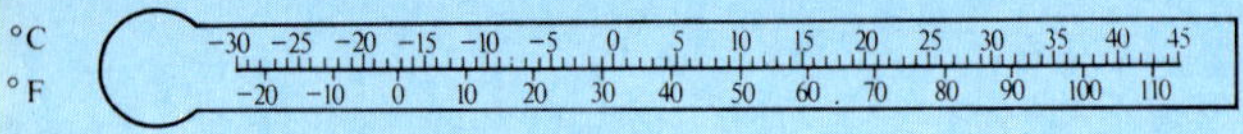

Length

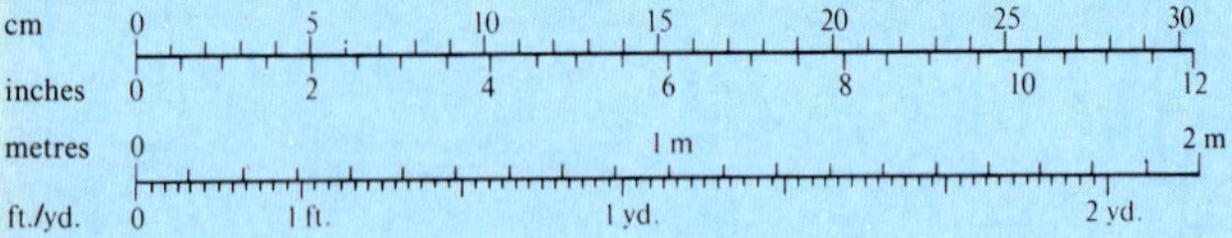

Weight

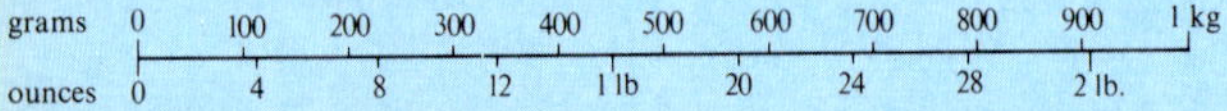

CRIME and THEFT. Though the Algarve has nothing resembling a crime wave, the Polícia de Segurança Publica (PSP) specifically warn tourists not to leave tempting objects visible in a parked car. Park your car in a guarded or well-lit place, they add, and lock it securely. Finally, don't leave your passport, personal documents, camera or other valuables in your tent or car.

Pick-pockets and purse-snatchers are not as prevalent in the Algarve as in Lisbon.

I want to report a theft. **Quero participar um roubo.**

D

DRIVING IN PORTUGAL. If you're driving to the Algarve, you need only your national driving licence, the car registration papers and the Green Card, an extension to the normal policy which makes it valid in other countries.

Driving conditions. The rules of the road are the same as in other European countries. You are obliged to wear seat-belts when driving or you risk a stiff fine. The roads of the Algarve—there are only a few kilometres of dual carriageway—are scarcely conducive to speeding. The dangers are many: Portuguese drivers, whose accident record is high; foreign drivers, stopping unexpectedly to seek directions or getting to know an unfamiliar rented car; and rustic obstructions like haycarts, tractors, donkeys and sheep that represent a particular hazard at night. Drivers entering roundabouts (traffic circles) normally have right of way. Children under 13 are not permitted to travel in the front seat.

Parking regulations. Unless there's an indication to the contrary, you can park as long as you wish. If marked, a sign will specify the maximum time you can stay. Parking meters haven't yet been discovered in the Algarve.

Speed limits. Unless otherwise posted, the limit is 90 kilometres per hour (56 m.p.h.) on normal highways and 60 k.p.h. (37 m.p.h.) in towns and built-up areas. On motorways/expressways it's 120 k.p.h. (75 m.p.h.). Cars towing caravans (trailers) are restricted to 50 k.p.h. (32 m.p.h.) in towns and 70 k.p.h. (43 m.p.h.) on the open road, also on motorways.

Fluid measures

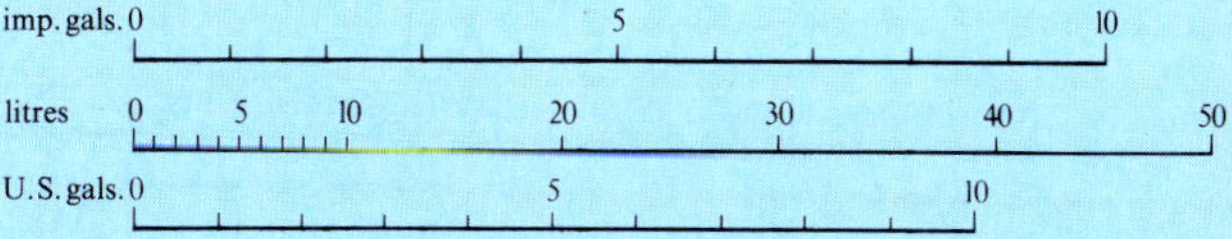

Distances. Here are some approximate road distances in kilometres between Faro and some provincial and regional centres:

Albufeira	40	Portimão	60
Alcantarilha	10	Porto	570
Ferreiras	35	Sagres	110
Lagoa	55	Silves	55
Lagos	75	Tavira	30
Lisbon	300	Vila Real de Santo António	50
Olhão	10		

To convert kilometres to miles:

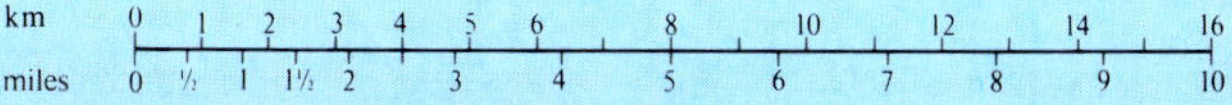

Traffic Police, see POLICE

Breakdowns. There are SOS telephones stationed about every three kilometres on the main highways. If you belong to a motoring organization affiliated with the Automóvel Clube de Portugal (ACP), you can make use of their emergency and repair services free of charge. ACP runs breakdown garages in Faro, Lagos and Portimão. Otherwise, most garages are equipped to handle the usual problems.

The emergency number for police and ambulance is 115 (free).

D

Road signs. The standard international picture-signs are used in Portugal, but you'll encounter some written notices as well. Among those you may see are:

Alto	Halt
Bermas baixas	Keep off the verge (Soft shoulder)
Cruzamento	Crossroads
Curva perigosa	Dangerous bend (curve)
Descida ingreme	Steep hill
Desvio	Diversion (Detour)
Encruzilhada	Crossroads
Estacionamento permitido	Parking allowed
Estacionamento proibido	No parking
Guiar com cuidado	Drive with care
Máquinas em manobras	Road works (Men working)
Obras	Road works (Men working)
Paragem de autocarro	Bus stop
Pare	Stop
Passagem proibida	No entry
Pedestres, peões	Pedestrians
Perigo	Danger
Posto de socorros	First-aid post
Proibida a entrada	No entry
Saída de camiões	Lorry (truck) exit
Seguir pela direita/esquerda	Keep right/left
Sem saída	No through road
Sentido proibido	No entry
Sentido único	One-way street
Silêncio	Silence zone
Trabalhos	Road works (Men working)
Trânsito proibido	No through traffic
Veículos pesados	Heavy vehicles
Velocidade máxima	Maximum speed
Zona de silêncio	Silence zone

Can I park here?	**Posso estacionar aqui?**
Are we on the right road for...?	**É esta a estrada para...?**
Fill the tank, please...	**Encha o depósito de..., por favor.**
normal/super	**normal/super**
Would you please change this tire?	**Pode mudar o pneu, por favor?**

D

Check the oil/tires/battery, please.	**Verifique o óleo/os pneus/ a bateria, se faz favor.**
I've had a breakdown.	**O meu carro está avariado.**
There's been an accident.	**Houve um acidente.**

DRUGS. Though certain drugs are widely disseminated among Portuguese and tourist youths, drug taking is illegal in Portugal, and the authorities take stern action against smugglers and traders.

E

ELECTRIC CURRENT. The standard current is 220-volt, 50-cycle A.C. Transformers and plug adaptors are required for American appliances.

I need an adaptor/a battery, please.	**Preciso de um adaptador/uma pilha, por favor.**

EMERGENCIES. The telephone number to dial in an emergency, anywhere in Portugal, is 115.

The hospitals at Albufeira, Faro, Lagos, Loulé, Olhão, Portimão and Vila Real de Santo António have *bancos de urgência* (emergency wards). Some hospitals can also handle dental emergencies. For trouble on the road, see under DRIVING.

ENTRY FORMALITIES and CUSTOMS CONTROLS *(alfândega).* American, British, Canadian and Irish citizens need only a valid passport—no visa—to visit Portugal, and even this requirement is waived for the British who may enter on the simplified Visitor's Passport. Though residents of Europe and North America aren't subject to any health requirements, visitors from further afield should check with a travel agent before departure in case any inoculation certificates are called for.

If you have nothing to declare, going through customs is as quick and easy as walking through the green channel. Here's what you can carry into Portugal duty-free and, upon your return home, into your own country:

E

Into:	Cigarettes		Cigars		Tobacco	Spirits		Wine
Portugal	200	or	50	or	250 g.*	1 l.	and	2 l.
Australia	200	or	250 g.	or	250 g.	1 l.	or	1 l.
Canada	200	and	50	and	900 g.	1.1 l.	or	1.1 l.
Eire	200	or	50	or	250 g.	1 l.	and	2 l.
N. Zealand	200	or	50	or	250 g.	1.1 l.	and	4.5 l.
S. Africa	400	and	50	and	250 g.	1 l.	and	2 l.
U.K.	200	or	50	or	250 g.	1 l.	and	2 l.
U.S.A.	200	and	100	and	**	1 l.	or	1 l.

* Residents of countries outside Europe may import double the quantity.
** A reasonable quantity.

In addition to personal clothing, jewellery and a small quantity of perfume, you are also allowed to take in a camera, a cine (movie) camera, a pair of binoculars, a portable radio and other items of a personal nature.

On departure you can buy spirits and tobacco at the airport's duty-free shop.

Currency restrictions: Visitors from abroad may take in or out of Portugal no more than 30,000 escudos. The amount of foreign currency you may take in either direction is unlimited, though you must declare anything over the equivalent of 50,000 escudos upon arrival.

I've nothing to declare. — **Não tenho nada a declarar.**
It's for my personal use. — **É para uso pessoal.**

G

GUIDES and INTERPRETERS. Several standard guided-tour itineraries are available through hotels and travel agencies. Qualified guides wear a badge with the seal of Portugal and the legend *Guia Turistica.*

If you need an interpreter for business purposes or an authorized guide for a non-organized tour, consult a travel agency in any of the resorts or towns of the Algarve.

We'd like an English-speaking guide/an English interpreter. — **Queremos um guia que fale inglês/um intérprete de inglês.**

HAIRDRESSERS*. Typical prices are far lower in neighbourhood salons in the towns than in the resorts and chic hotels. Men's barbers are called *barbeiros*, women's and unisex salons, *cabeleireiros*. For tipping suggestions, see TIPPING.

The following vocabulary will help:

I'd like a shampoo and set.	**Queria um champô e mise.**
I want a...	**Quero...**
haircut	**um corte**
razor cut	**um corte à navalha**
blow-dry (brushing)	**um brushing**
permanent wave	**uma permanente**
colour chart	**um mostruário de cores**
colour rinse	**uma rinsage**
manicure	**uma manicura**
Don't cut it too short.	**Não corte muito curto.**
A little more off (here).	**Corte mais um pouco (aqui).**

HITCH-HIKING. In the Algarve hitch-hiking is quite common—and effective. But it's unwise to try it after dark: drivers are less likely to stop, and there's always the possibility of danger.

Can you give me/us a lift to...?	**Pode levar-me/-nos a ...?**

HOTELS and ACCOMMODATION*. See also CAMPING and YOUTH HOSTELS. Hotels *(hotel)* throughout Portugal are officially inspected and classified with one to five stars. In the Algarve there are several other types of accommodation, also regulated by the government: a "touristic village" has villas and apartments rated up to three stars, with a "luxury" classification on top. An *estalagem* (inn) is usually simpler and smaller than a hotel of the same category. A *pensão*, rated from one to three stars, is a boarding house charging far less than a hotel. State-run *pousadas* (similar to the Spanish *paradores*) are installed in scenic castles or convents or in out-of-the-way locations tourists might otherwise miss. With *O Turismo de Habitação*, dozens of castles, manors and country houses have been opened up by their owners, under the aegis of the government, providing magnificent accommodation in refined surroundings. Each has been restored in its traditional style and architecture. The Portuguese National Tourist Office (see TOURIST INFORMATION OFFICES) will be able to provide the latest up-to-date list.

H

When you arrive at your hotel, inn or boarding house you'll receive a form which sets out the conditions, prices and room number. The price includes continental breakfast.

I'd like a single/double room.	**Queria um quarto simples/duplo.**
with bath/shower	**com banho/chuveiro**
What's the rate per night?	**Qual é o preço por noite?**

L

LANGUAGE. In the Algarve a sing-song version of Portuguese is used. Your high school Spanish may help you read signs and menus but will not unlock the mysteries of the spoken language. But almost all Portuguese understand Spanish. And in the Algarve English is widely understood.

The Berlitz phrasebook PORTUGUESE FOR TRAVELLERS covers most of the situations you're likely to encounter during a visit to Portugal. Also useful is the Portuguese-English/English-Portuguese pocket dictionary, containing a special menu-reader supplement.

A few words to get you going:

Good morning	**Bom dia**
Good evening	**Boa noite**
Please	**Por favor**
Thank you	**Obrigado/Obrigada** (fem.)
Good-bye	**Adeus**
Yes/No	**Sim/Não**
Do you speak English?	**Fala inglês?**
I don't speak Portuguese.	**Não falo português.**

LAUNDRY and DRY-CLEANING. Hotels accept clothing for dry-cleaning and laundry service, which is good and reasonably fast. Three-day service is common, but one-day express service is also available at extra cost. Self-service launderettes are uncommon. For addresses of laundries and cleaners, look in the classified telephone directory under "Lavandarias e Tinturarias".

Where's the nearest laundry/dry-cleaner's?	**Onde fica a lavandaria/lavandaria a seco mais próxima?**
When will it be ready?	**Quando estará pronto?**
I must have this for tomorrow morning.	**Preciso disto para amanhã de manhã.**

L

LOST PROPERTY. Generally the nearest police station is the place to go to report lost property. If you lose something on a bus, though, you might start at the bus terminal. There is no central clearing house for lost property.

I've lost my...	**Perdi...**
wallet/bag/passport	**a minha carteira/o meu saco/ o meu passaporte**

M

MAPS. The tourist office has free brochures including a map of the Algarve and simple plans of the principal towns. For more detailed road maps go to a bookstore or news-stand. The Automóvel Clube de Portugal issues a comprehensive map of the country.

a street map of...	**uma planta de...**
a road map of the Algarve	**um mapa das estradas do Algarve**

MEDICAL CARE. See also EMERGENCIES. All the principal towns of the Algarve have their own hospitals; many have doctors who know foreign languages. Any local tourist office has a list of doctors and dentists who speak English.

Medical insurance to cover the risk of illness or accident while abroad is a worthwhile investment. Your travel agent or regular insurance company will have modestly priced policies.

Farmácias (pharmacies) are open during normal business hours. In addition, one pharmacy in every town is always on duty around the clock. Its address is announced on the door of every other *farmácia*.

In the heat of summer, take the sun in small doses until your skin acquires a bit of tan. On certain beaches the wet sand may harbour a tiny creature called the *peixe-aranha* (weever—literally, spider-fish). Stepping on one could result in a very painful bite.

Where's the nearest (all-night) pharmacy?	**Onde fica a farmácia (de serviço) mais próxima?**
I need a doctor/dentist.	**Preciso de um médico/dentista.**
an ambulance	**uma ambulância**
hospital	**hospital**
sunburn	**queimadura de sol**
sunstroke	**uma insolação**
a fever	**febre**
an upset stomach	**dôr de estômago**
insect bite	**uma picadela de insecto**

MEETING PEOPLE. The Portuguese are shy, so you may have to take the first step if you want to make friends. They'll react very warmly to your initiative. As everywhere, young people are more spontaneous and outgoing. People are less reserved at beaches and cafés than most other places. If you're really serious about wanting to get close to the Portuguese, the tourist office can find you lodging in a local household.

Don't let it bother you if people, especially villagers, seem to be staring at you; it's only unaffected curiosity. On the other hand, it's sometimes difficult to catch the eye of a waiter when you need him. The Portuguese have no equivalent for "Waiter!" but use the term *Faz favor* (Please!).

How do you do?	**Muito prazer.**
How are you?	**Como está?**
Very well, thank you.	**Muito bem, obrigado/ obrigada** (fem.).

MONEY MATTERS

Currency. Don't be appalled when you see price tags quoting many digits punctuated by the $ sign. Here it means *escudo* (abbreviated *esc.*), not dollar; the sign normally replaces the decimal point (thus 5.000$00 means 5,000 escudos). The escudo is divided into 100 *centavos.* Coins of 10 and 20 centavos rarely come a tourist's way, but the 50-centavo coin (*cinco tostões* in slang) is common along with 1-, 2½- and 5-escudo coins. There is also a rare 10-escudo and a new 25-escudo coin. Banknotes come in denominations of 20, 50, 100, 500, 1,000 and 5,000 escudos. For currency restrictions, see ENTRY FORMALITIES AND CUSTOMS CONTROLS.

Banking hours are from 8.30 to 11.45 a.m. and 1 to 2.45 p.m., Monday to Friday.

After hours and on Saturdays one bank or another in the big towns stays open during the height of the tourist season; the exchange office at Faro airport stays open until the last major flight of the evening. Your hotel will also change money, but at a less favourable rate.

Traveller's cheques are easily cashed but be sure to take your passport with you for identification.

Credit cards of the well-known international companies are accepted in major hotels, restaurants and tourist-orientated enterprises as well as in car hire agencies.

M

Prices. Compared with North European or American prices, things aren't notably expensive in Portugal—with two major exceptions, cars and the fuel to run them. Of course, everything is less in non-tourist establishments. Certain rates are listed on page 103 to give you an idea of what things cost.

Haggling is not done; prices are as marked.

Where's the nearest bank/ currency exchange office?	**Onde fica o banco mais próximo/ a casa de câmbio mais próxima?**
I want to change some pounds/ dollars.	**Queria trocar libras/dólares.**
Can I cash a traveller's cheque?	**Posso trocar um cheque de viagem?**
Can I pay with this credit card?	**Posso pagar com este cartão de crédito?**
How much is that?	**Quanto custa isto?**

N

NEWSPAPERS and MAGAZINES *(jornal; revista).* Europe's principal newspapers, including most British dailies and the *International Herald Tribune* are available on the day after publication at many newsagents and hotels. Popular foreign magazines are sold at the same shops or stands. Paperback books in English are on sale everywhere.

For tourists, the monthly *Algarve Magazine,* in English, includes useful information, addresses, telephone numbers and announcements of coming events.

Have you any English-language newspapers/magazines?	**Tem jornais/revistas em inglês?**

P

PHOTOGRAPHY. Well-known brands of film in all sizes are sold at photo shops, news-stands and many other outlets. Black and white film can be processed in 24 hours but colour takes several days in Faro and longer in the resorts. Since the processing costs are high in Portugal, it may be worthwhile taking your exposed films home undeveloped.

Aside from places where one could possibly be photographing "military secrets", e.g. airports, docks, there are normally no restrictions on what you may film.

I'd like a film for this camera.	**Quero um rolo para esta máquina.**
a black-and-white film	**um rolo a preto e branco**
a colour film	**um rolo a cores**
a colour-slide film	**um rolo de diapositivos**

P

35-mm film	**um rolo de trinta e cinco milímetros**
super-8	**super oito**
How long will it take to develop this film?	**Quanto tempo leva a revelar este filme?**
May I take a picture?	**Posso tirar uma fotografia?**

POLICE *(polícia)*. In resorts and towns with tourist traffic, look for the police wearing armbands marked "CD" (for *Corpo Distrital*, or local corps). They are assigned to assist tourists; normally they speak one or more foreign languages.

On highways, traffic is controlled by the Guarda Nacional Republicana (GNR) in white cars or on motorcycles. Occasionally they make spot checks on documents or the condition of tires. The way to address any policeman is "Senhor Guarda".

Where's the nearest police station?	**Onde fica o posto de polícia mais próximo?**

PUBLIC HOLIDAYS *(feriado)*

Jan. 1	*Ano Novo*	New Year's Day
April 25	*Dia de Portugal*	National Day
May 1	*Dia do Trabalho*	Labour Day
June 10	*Dia de Camões*	Camoens' Day
Aug. 15	*Assunção*	Assumption
Oct. 5	*Dia da República*	Republic Day
Nov. 1	*Todos-os-Santos*	All Saints' Day
Dec. 1	*Restauração*	Restoration Day (of Independence)
Dec. 8	*Imaculada Conceição*	Immaculate Conception
Dec. 25	*Natal*	Christmas Day
Movable dates:	*Sexta-feira Santa*	Good Friday
	Corpo de Deus	Corpus Christi

These are only the *national* holidays of Portugal. Many special holidays affect different branches of the economy or regions of the country. And every town closes down at least one day a year in honour of its own patron saint.

Are you open tomorrow?	**Estão abertos amanhã?**

RADIO and TV *(radio; televisão)*. Only one of Portugal's two government-operated TV channels is relayed to the Algarve. But in some parts of the region Spanish television comes in clearly, too. The Portuguese channel shows a good many foreign films, with the sound-track in the original language and subtitles in Portuguese.

Except for Radio Renascença, a station owned by the Catholic church, all Portuguese radio stations are operated by the government. Radio Algarve broadcasts news in English in the morning and early evening.

Spanish and Moroccan programmes also are clearly audible on ordinary transistors along the coast. Short wave sets pick up the Voice of America, BBC, Radio Canada International—even Radio Australia—as well as the principal European stations.

RELIGIOUS SERVICES *(serviço religioso)*. The overwhelming majority of Portuguese are Roman Catholics. Services in English are scheduled in principal tourist areas. Protestant (primarily Anglican) services are held in several localities along the coast. All tourist offices and almost all hotels have a list of the religious services available in the area.

SHOPPING HOURS. Most shops and offices are open from 9 a.m. to 1 p.m. and 3 to 7 p.m., Monday to Friday, and from 9 a.m. to 1 p.m. on Saturdays. The siesta, so much a part of life just across the border in Spain, is not observed here; but two hours for lunch is the norm.

TIME DIFFERENCES. In winter Portugal observes Greenwich Mean Time (GMT). In summer, the clock is put one hour ahead:

New York	London	**Algarve**	Jo'burg	Sydney	Auckland
7 a.m.	noon	**noon**	1 p.m.	9 p.m.	11 p.m.

What time is it, please? **Que horas são, por favor?**

TIPPING. Hotel and restaurant bills are generally all-inclusive, though waiters are given an additional tip if service has been good. It is also in order to hand the bellboys, doormen, hat check attendants, filling-station attendants, etc., a coin or two for their service.

The following chart suggests how much to leave:

Hairdresser/Barber	10%
Hotel maid, per week	200 esc.
Lavatory attendant	25 esc.
Hotel porter, per bag	50 esc.
Taxi driver	10%
Tour guide	10–15%
Waiter	10% (optional)

TOILETS *(lavabos/toiletes).* The most likely places to find clean facilities are in hotels and restaurants, though public conveniences are established in busy town centres. If there's an attendant on duty, a coin or two would be an appreciated gesture. "Ladies" is *Senhoras* and "Gentlemen", *Homens.*

Where are the toilets? **Onde ficam os toiletes?**

TOURIST INFORMATION OFFICES *(oficio do turismo).* The Portuguese government maintains tourist offices in more than a dozen foreign countries. Here are some addresses:

Canada: Suite 704, Canada Square, 2200 Young Street, Toronto, Ont. M4S 2C6; tel. (416) 364-8133.

1801 McGill College Avenue, Montreal, Que. H3A 2N4; tel. (514) 282-1264.

Great Britain: New Bond Street House, 1–5, New Bond Street, London W1Y ODB; tel. (01) 493-3873.

U.S.A.: 548 Fifth Avenue, New York, NY 10036; tel. (212) 354-4403.

Suite 3001, 969 Michigan Avenue, Chicago, IL 60611; tel. (312) 266-9898.

Suite 616, 3640 Wilshire Boulevard, Los Angeles, CA 90010; tel. (213) 580-6459.

In the Algarve itself there are more than a dozen tourist information offices staffed by multilingual personnel who provide brochures and information on local conditions.

TRANSPORT

Buses *(autocarro).* The state-run Rodoviaria Nacional (R.N.) organization operates most buses in the Algarve. A few vehicles assigned to remote local services are rickety but most are modern and comfortable. A baffling variety of local and regional timetables may be consulted at any bus station or tourist information office. Most buses keep the announced schedule fairly punctually.

Some buses board through the front door, others through the rear. Since there is no way of predicting, just look for the sign *Entrada* over one of the doors. (*Saída* means exit.) If you don't pass a conductor seated behind a little desk near the entrance of the bus, it means you are to take a seat and wait for him to come around to accept your fare. One exception: on buses of the Algarve Express service, tickets must be bought in advance at bus stations.

Bus stops are identified by a sign reading *Paragem.*

Inter-city buses. Rodoviaria Nacional and some private firms run express coaches linking Algarve towns and resorts with Lisbon. Some have air-conditioning and other amenities. Travel agencies can provide timetables, information and reservations.

Taxis *(táxi).* All Portuguese taxis are black cars with green roofs. In the Algarve the letter "A"—for *aluguer* (for hire)—is prominently marked on the front doors. Taxis don't normally cruise for business but wait for customers at specific taxi ranks—at least one in each town and tourist resort. In the high season you may well find the taxi rank empty for a few minutes or even longer. If you have an important appointment it's worthwhile to arrange for the taxi in advance.

Taxis in the Algarve have no meters but follow a standard fare table based on mileage. Tipping is by no means obligatory, but drivers don't object to a bonus.

Trains *(combóio).* A railway line runs from Lagos in the west to the eastern frontier at Vila Real de Santo António. Stations are in or near the main towns, but sometimes far enough away to require a bus or taxi ride. Most notable, the railway station called Albufeira is near Ferreiras, a 15-minute bus ride from the resort; the bus and train schedules are not apparently synchronized. There is no great difference in time or price between long-distance buses and trains, but the railway line offers more unspoiled scenery.

Many trains have both first- and second-class carriages. A first-class carriage usually has a distinguishing yellow stripe above the windows and a number "1" near the doors. There are no restaurant cars on Algarve trains.

T

A railway line links the Algarve with Lisbon. The fastest trains take three hours to cover the distance between the Algarve junction Tunes, and Barreiro, across the Tagus river from Lisbon. (The ferry-boat is included in the price of the train ticket.)

Where is the railway station/the nearest bus stop?	**Onde é a estação ferroviária/a paragem de autocarros mais próxima?**
When's the next bus/train to...?	**Quando parte o próximo autocarro/combóio para...?**
I want a ticket to...	**Queria um bilhete para...**
single (one-way)	**ida**
return (round-trip)	**ida e volta**
first/second class	**primeira/segunda classe**
Will you tell me when to get off?	**Pode dizer-me quando devo descer?**
Where can I get a taxi?	**Onde posso encontrar um táxi?**
What's the fare to...?	**Quanto custa o percurso para...?**

W

WATER *(água).* Problems with tap water have arisen in certain towns. Though on the whole the water is safe to drink, you would do best to stick to bottled mineral water, sold everywhere at reasonable prices. The Algarve's own source of mineral water is Monchique. Water from Monchique comes bottled in still and fizzy varieties.

In a small village you might see a fountain marked *Esta água deve ser fervida* ("This water must be boiled").

a bottle of mineral water	**uma garrafa de água mineral**
fizzy (carbonated)/still	**com/sem gás**

Y

YOUTH HOSTELS. Young tourists from 14 up can stay in dormitories at very low rates if they're members of a national or international youth hostel association. Membership in the Portuguese Youth Hostel Association is open to "juniors" (aged 14 to 21) and "seniors" (22 to 40). Parents with children younger than 14 may, in certain cases, stay in these hostels if there is room, but preference is given to those within the set age brackets. The headquarters of the Portuguese Youth Hostel Association *(Associação Portuguesa de Pousadas de Juventude)* is at:

Rua Andrade Corvo, 46, Lisbon; tel. 571054.

Is there a youth hostel near here?	**Há alguma pousada de juventude aqui perto?**

SOME USEFUL EXPRESSIONS

yes/no	**sim/não**
please/thank you	**faz favor/obrigado (obrigada)**
excuse me/you're welcome	**perdão/de nada**
where/when/how	**onde/quando/como**
how long/how far	**quanto tempo/a que distância**
yesterday/today/tomorrow	**ontem/hoje/amanhã**
day/week/month/year	**dia/semana/mês/ano**
left/right	**esquerdo/direito**
good/bad	**bom/mau**
big/small	**grande/pequeno**
cheap/expensive	**barato/caro**
hot/cold	**quente/frio**
old/new	**velho/novo**
open/closed	**aberto/fechado**
up/down	**em cima/em baixo**
here/there	**aqui/ali**
free (vacant)/occupied	**livre/ocupado**
early/late	**cedo/tarde**
easy/difficult	**fácil/difícil**
Does anyone here speak English?	**Alguém fala inglês?**
What does this mean?	**Que quer dizer isto?**
I don't understand.	**Não compreendo.**
Please write it down.	**Escreva-mo, por favor.**
Is there an admission charge?	**Paga-se entrada?**
Waiter!/Waitress!	**Faz favor!**
I'd like…	**Queria…/Quero…**
How much is that?	**Quanto custa isto?**
Have you something less expensive?	**Tem qualquer coisa de mais barato?**
Just a minute.	**Um momento.**
What time is it?	**Que horas são?**
Help me, please.	**Ajude-me, por favor.**
Get a doctor, quickly.	**Chame um médico, depressa.**

Index

An asterisk (*) next to a page number indicates a map reference. For index to Practical Information, see also page 104.

INDEX

158/611 SUD